THE INDIANA HOME

Don Leslie

1-765-662-
3843

gift from
Sandra Dolby

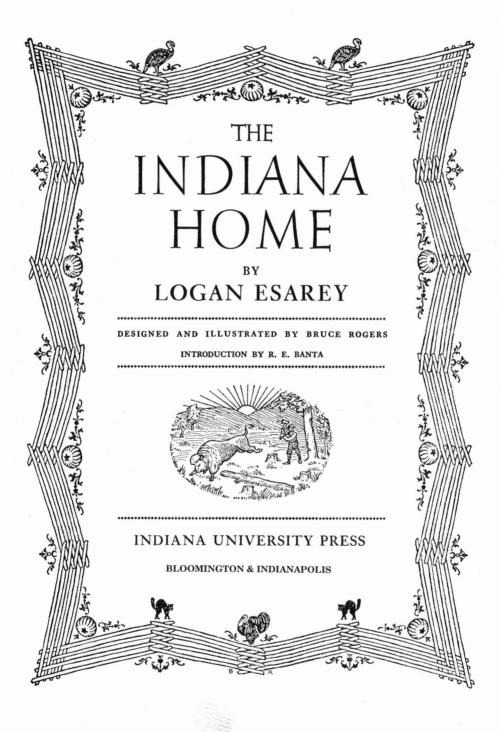

THE
INDIANA
HOME

BY
LOGAN ESAREY

DESIGNED AND ILLUSTRATED BY BRUCE ROGERS

INTRODUCTION BY R. E. BANTA

INDIANA UNIVERSITY PRESS

BLOOMINGTON & INDIANAPOLIS

Published in Canada by Fitzhenry & Whiteside Limited,
Don Mills, Ontario
Manufactured in the United States of America

Library of Congress Cataloging in Publication Data
Esarey, Logan, 1873–1942.
The Indiana home.
1. Pioneer and frontier life—Indiana. 2. Indiana—
Social life and customs. I. Rogers, Bruce, 1870–1957.
II. Title.
ISBN 0-253-32016-X
ISBN 0-253-20742-8 (pbk.)

1 2 3 4 5   96 95 94 93 92

ESAREY'S BOYHOOD HOME

INTRODUCTION

TODAY there is no living professor of history who can write about the Midwestern pioneer farm life from his own experience. The last person who could and did do so was probably Logan Esarey, a professor at Indiana University, who died September 24, 1942, and who wrote the sketches in this volume.

Dr. Esarey was born in 1873 near Branchville, Perry County, in the heart of the Indiana "Knob Country"—at that time and for many years to come this area was about as backward as any that could be found in the state. He was one of the eight children (one died in infancy) of John Clark and Barbara Ewing Esarey. The family home was a two-room log cabin, later enlarged by a two-story addition also of logs; and the small farm was neither fertile nor otherwise prosperous: it was, in fact, a typical "family farm" of the day, the passing of which is now bewailed by romantic souls and "bleeding hearts" who never suffered the strain of trying to win a family living from one of them.

The Esarey farm was in no way modern,

i

even for its day. It was probably operated much as it had been in Logan Esarey's grandfather's time, with Logan employed as a full-time farmhand from about the time he started to school. Thus he knew the skills of hand cultivation and he was experienced in the chores that were necessary to powerless frontier farming: from cultivating by hoe and hand-shucking corn to carrying water from spring to kitchen and toting out household waste to slop the hogs. Certainly he early learned the pleasures and pitfalls of chopping and splitting firewood for cooking and heating and the endless task of carrying the finished product into the house and the ashes out. Besides, he knew from observation if not from participation something of the finer points of frontier housekeeping. As an importunate three-year-old, he had first been allowed to help his mother and sisters with post-prandial rites by drying dishes fresh from the scalding water in the dishpan on the kitchen table (being third- or fourth-generation Hoosier settlers, the family probably referred to this operation as "wiping dishes"). Possibly his mother used a spinning wheel—if not, some female relative or neighbor woman certainly did. Somewhere he saw wool or linen being spun, and by the time he was four he knew how far apart to hold his hands to receive the finished yarn for skeining.

Work was endless on the few acres that supported from nine to ten in the family, plus whatever number of kinfolk had stopped in to stay a few days—or months, or years. Work began well before sunup and continued far into the night.

It was not the kind of labor that showed a monetary profit either. So, when young Logan decided that he would continue his education beyond the few years offered by the neighborhood grade school—might even go to college— he was pretty much on his own as far as financial assistance was concerned. He began in the same way as many another youth with leanings toward higher education: armed with whatever knowledge he had picked up in his six or seven years of schooling, he himself became a teacher in a local village school. He was sixteen years old!

After three years he took what must have been meagre savings from his salary of two or three hundred dollars a year, and he entered Danville Normal School at Danville, Indiana. As was the custom in normal schools of his day, he combined what would now be a course of high school studies with work at college level when he was advanced enough for it, and so he got his first taste of liberal arts and the classics. He continued to study at Danville, taking a year or two off now and then to teach again in grade schools in order to bolster his finances, until he eventually raised his sights and decided to work toward a college degree, and possibly go on to advanced study after that. In 1903 he enrolled at Indiana University, where in 1905 he received his A.B. degree. Later, after time out for more teaching and work in school administration to

earn funds, he received his A.M. and Ph.D. de-
grees. It was probably during the years of his
studies at Indiana University, with the opportunity for wider reading in a library with far more
books than Danville Normal's had, that Esarey
became aware of the fact, true at the time, that
most texts on Midwestern history, and indeed
most books on the subject, had been written by
citizens of the Eastern seaboard. Esarey did not
agree with the views of these scholarly but unin-
formed gentlemen. He knew some of the people
who had settled Indiana and a great many of
their first- and second-generation descendants.
They were not as they had been all too often described in Eastern books. Later he said of them,
"They were not poor white trash, as Eastern
historians would have it; they were the salt of
the earth and their like never will be seen on the
face of the earth again."

It may have been his resentment of the real or
fancied prejudices of the historical establishment
of the day that caused Logan Esarey to reflect
that he, and possibly he alone of the current students in the field, was one who had *known* the
pioneers and had watched and practiced their
way of life. He could explain and defend them
and their ways. The hardships he had known
and undergone in his youth were not suffered in
vain: his observations and experiences, passed on
to his students, would give a new dimension to
Midwestern history. In the words of the frontier, Esarey "had been thar when it happened";
he "had seed the elephant"; and he could "tell it

like it wuz!" The direction of his scholarship and his teaching was set; it would continue throughout his life, and it would inspire alike the casual, none-too-bright underclassman and the earnest graduate student.

Eighteen ninety-seven was a big year: he laid the foundations for his own continuing education by accepting the post of superintendent of the Perry County schools (a position he held until 1903), and on May 20 he married Laura Pearson. He followed his years of service in Perry County with a stint, between 1907 and 1909, as principal of the Vincennes high school and later the Bloomington high school; and from 1909 to 1912 he served as dean of Winona College at Warsaw, Indiana.

In the fall of 1911 Esarey became a faculty member in the Department of History at Indiana University—the next spring he received his doctorate—and continued his teaching there until his retirement. Always a pithy and entertaining lecturer, he introduced several new courses as time went on: one in Indiana history, probably the first offered anywhere at college level, for instance, and another on the history of the Midwest—certainly the first time Dr. Esarey's beloved homeland had been so signally recognized. He was also much in demand throughout the state as a speaker for nonacademic occasions, and he was considered by his contemporaries to be one of the best representatives to the general public the university had ever had. As personally aware as he was of the vocabulary and attitude of both the plowman and the academician, he could hardly fail to win the approval and respect of any audience in the area. As he himself said, his father and grandfather had "hunted bears and Indians in seven states" and in time had found their way to Indiana from Kentucky, Virginia, and Tennessee.

Dr. Esarey did not spend all his time lecturing, either to students or to citizens outside his classrooms. He contributed to learned journals frequently and published a number of pamphlets in his field of scholarship. For several years he edited the *Indiana Magazine of History*, published by the Indiana Historical Society. He also wrote some excellent books: among them *History of Indiana from the Earliest Exploration to the Present*, which was published in two volumes in 1915–1918, thus coinciding with the state's centennial in 1916; and in 1927, with Charles E. Finch, he coauthored *The Government of Indiana*.

Dr. Esarey did not intend *The Indiana Home*, of which this is the fourth edition, to be a book; it is composed of essays found among his papers after his death on September 24, 1942, and had evidently been written to be used as lectures or to entertain and instruct his grandchildren.

Besides his teaching and writing, Dr. Esarey continually sought out diaries and other manuscripts, files of early newspapers, pamphlets, and any other material relating to his beloved Midwestern pioneers, and added his finds to the Indiana University Library, thus helping to lay the foundation for what has come to be, after many millions of dollars in gifts and contributions, one of the greatest and most important historical collections in the world today.

Retiring in 1941, Dr. Esarey enjoyed his emeritus status less than a year—if he actually did enjoy such an inactive state—before his death in the fall of the next year. He had taught at the university almost forty years, during which time he had instilled in the minds of his students a much clearer idea of the problems of pioneer life and a much sounder picture of the actual process by which the frontier had developed than they could have acquired from anyone else at the time.

* * *

The format of the present volume and the pen-and-ink drawings which illustrate it are the work of another talented Hoosier, the distinguished typographer Bruce Rogers. Mr. Rogers was born in Lafayette, Indiana, in 1870, a son of George and Anna Gish Rogers. After attending local schools, he entered Purdue University. He and John T. McCutcheon, who was later to become a famous newpaper humorist and cartoonist, are said to have been the only two male students enrolled in the school's art classes. Rogers received his B.S. degree in 1890. The years from 1882 to 1890 must have been lively ones at Purdue. In addition to Rogers and McCutcheon, both George Barr and Ben F. McCutcheon (John T.'s brothers), as well as

INTRODUCTION

George Ade and Booth Tarkington were enrolled there for varying periods of time. All of them became writers and published books, some of which were tremendously successful. That must have been an unusual decade in an institution whose chief aim has always been to produce various types of engineers and agriculturists.

After graduation Bruce Rogers found employment on the art staff of the *Indianapolis News*, then the state's leading newspaper. Later he also worked for the periodical *Modern Art;* and when its place of publication was moved to Boston in 1895, Rogers went along. While working for *Modern Art* he had become interested in the then neglected art of book design; and, once located in Boston, he soon found employment as a book designer for the Riverside Press of Houghton Mifflin and Company, a leading American publishing house—an establishment which coincidentally had published many of those works by the Eastern historians whose views of the frontier Logan Esarey rejected. Rogers did not share Dr. Esarey's active animosity toward these gentlemen, but he had been born early enough and close enough to the frontier to appreciate Esarey's views; and when, late in Rogers' life, an opportunity came to plan and illustrate an edition of *The Indiana Home*, he welcomed it and undertook the work in his eighty-third year.

From 1895, when he joined Houghton Mifflin, until his death on May 18, 1957, Rogers (who generally signed his works "Bruce Rogers of Indiana") designed books, great and small— often the works of the world's greatest writers —for many leading publishers. His work was by no means limited to laying out page form, specifying typefaces, and selecting type ornaments —which is the extent of the efforts of many book designers. Rogers was competent with pen or pencil and was able to create himself the kind of design he wished to use. He originated a number of new typefaces, some of which were so successful that they have been adopted by type founders. In recognition of his work Rogers eventually received, among other important awards, the gold medal of the American Institute of Arts and Letters.

This little book, then, is the joint effort of two proud Hoosiers: Esarey set out to correct the ideas of Eastern seaboard historians because those writers seemed to believe that the Midwest had been settled by "poor white trash"—when really the early adventurers had been "the salt of the earth . . . whose like will never be seen again." Bruce Rogers, who had also known folk of the pioneer strain and who signed himself "Bruce Rogers *of Indiana*," agreed with him.

I trust I may be pardoned if I sign this introduction as a more obscure but no less dedicated Hoosier,

R. E. BANTA

THE INDIANA HOME

Indian Huts

THE FIRST INHABITANTS

The first inhabitants of what is now Indiana were almost savage Indians. They numbered only a few thousands, probably as many as there are now white people in our smallest county. They lived in little huts such as they could build with their bare hands. They had no tools of iron. With sharp stones they could cut bark from the birch tree, they could cure or tan a few buffalo-, deer-, and bearskins, and they could burn a few small logs or poles to convenient lengths with which they did their building.

At Fort Wayne or Miamitown on the Miami, on Eel River, at Lafayette or the Weatown on the Wabash, on the Vermillion and elsewhere, they had what they called ancestral towns. These consisted of a few shacks and maybe a totem pole. The totem was a hardwood pole on the top of which with a sharp rock and fire they had carved some kind of a rude image of a bird, wolf, turtle, or whatever animal they thought they were descended from, reminding us of our supposed ape and monkey ancestors. Around these poles they would gather at stated times and hold their tribal feasts and ceremonies. Dressed to resemble buffaloes, deer, bears or wolves they would gather at night by a blazing bonfire and sing and dance. Each warrior in turn would enter the ring and

3

hop around and yelp, boasting how many war-riors he had killed. Then he would grab his war club and kill a few imaginary enemies to show how it was done. When he had "run down" an-other would leap into the ring and go through the whole performance again. Thus the night was spent. The old missionaries who often watched them said they acted like demons. I should think they would more resemble a pack of tom-cats in a dark alley. In later years when the tomahawk and scalping knife took the place of the war club the whole performance ended in a drunken jamboree. American missionaries who watched them said more Indians were killed in these drunken debauches than in all the wars with white men.

These, however, were the noble red men at their worst. Ordinarily they lived in small groups of three or four families. While the squaws cul-tivated their little patches of corn, beans, pump-kins and squashes, at least one man was scouting the trails for approaching enemies, one or two were hunting or fishing, while one or two basked lazily around in the sunshine, sleeping with one eye and ear open for any sight or sound of danger. Like all uncivilized men, and some civilized, the men never interfered in the farm or housework. The papooses, each in his tiny sack or cradle, hung on their mothers' backs or on convenient limbs. The children with their pack of dogs played in the neighborhood and became expert in catching small game, fish and turtles. They ate what they had and made no complaint. If a deer or bear were killed they ate all they could before it spoiled, fed the remainder to the dogs and then ate the dogs.

Some of the corn, beans and dried pumpkins could be saved for the winter. In the autumn there were nuts and wild fruits and plenty of game. When cold winter set in they selected a place protected from the winter storm and prepared to "tough it out," fortunate if some did not freeze or starve.

Nature was a puzzle to these simple minds and each year found them as unprepared as the last. Two spirits, the North Wind and the South Wind, struggled continuously. When the North Wind prevailed, the fish gathered in the deep pools, the lubberly bears crawled into hollow trees and went to sleep, the deer sought the sunny slopes of the southern hills and even the big simple buffaloes gathered in long lines and lazily strolled off to the bluegrass and canebrakes of Kentucky, then a part of Virginia. Their trail, cut deep in the loose soil of the forest, may still be seen near Jasper, French Lick or Paoli. Many of the Indians, divided into bands of four or five families, followed slowly to the protecting hills and cliffs near the Ohio River and prepared their winter wigwams. As the cruel North Wind covered the land with his icy breath, the women and children housed up and the hunters followed the game to Kentucky, returning from time to time with what meat they could obtain. Thus had these simple folks spent centuries in Indiana before any white man ever entered their home. They certainly were not making any progress in civilization and it seems certain that they were decreasing in number.

Into this Indian land about three centuries ago came strange white men, some dressed in peaked wool caps, shirts and colored capotes with leggings and buckskin moccasins and some dressed in long black robes of foreign cloth and wearing shining ornaments of gold and glass. These were the French hunters and traders, known in history as *coureurs de bois* or *voyageurs*, and the missionaries. The former had flintlock muskets with which they could kill game much more easily and certainly than the Indians could with bow and arrow. They had steel fish hooks which made it easy for even the children to catch fish; they had long, sharp hunting knives with which they could skin the bear, deer or beaver and cut them into convenient pieces for cooking or drying; they had steel hatchets or tomahawks with which they could cut firewood and logs for stockades and huts; they had iron pots and pans in which they could really cook all kinds of food—as we say in the books "stone" men meeting "iron" men.

The missionaries were a still greater puzzle to the Indians. They had no weapons, would not fight, had no enemies and did not care to trade. They taught the women and children how to use the strange iron implements, showed them how to build new houses, to improve their farming and keep the house. They had some simple medicines and remedies for the sick. Not many of the missionaries came to Indiana, but their teachings were brought by the Indians who visited Canada in large numbers and especially by the Wyandot Indians, formerly Hurons, who came down to the Maumee Valley and who had known the French for a century.

When George Croghan visited the Wea towns in 1764 the Indians there lived in log cabins clustered around a stockade trading post. They had carried white sand up from the water's edge for their floors and each family seems to have had its own house. Out on the prairie they had large fields of corn well cultivated with the new iron hoes brought by the French traders. These same traders had taught them how to cure their furs and hides so they would pass on the French market. Each Indian wore at least some cloth clothing. With their sharp hatchets it was no trick to make the birch canoes and now each warrior and most of the boys owned one. Instead of a three months' hunting trip down across the state to the Ohio River they could jump in their canoes and be on the Ohio in twenty-four hours. From there they could paddle leisurely up the Green, the Salt or the Cumberland to almost any part of Kentucky carrying back venison for the winter's use.

The boys who were too small to go on the long hunt could catch any amount of fish with their steel hooks and steelshod gigs. There were bushels of walnuts, hickory nuts, hazel nuts, and acorns to store away in the log huts. Besides, from the time the corn was in roasting ear until it was gathered the girls had to keep the crows and wild pigeons out by day and the boys and dogs had to keep out deer, bears and coons by night.

Moreover, autumn was a busy season for the squaws. They had learned the use of many plants in cooking. Some were used for spices, some for seasoning but most of them were for their medical practice. They were skillful in all first-aid treatments and in treating minor ills. Whether they had learned this from experience or from the Catholic missionaries is not clear. These priests were the best educated men in the world at the time and it is more than probable that some of the

7

herb remedies used by squaws on the Wabash came from the Botanical Gardens of the Grand Monarch in Paris.

As further evidence of their improvement they had developed a large number of medical quacks much as we have. There was one or more in each village who could cure the sick by sorcery or magic. He proceeded to dress himself in some animal skin, preferably with horns and tail, took the patient into his little lodge, howled, beat the tom-tom, rattled the magic bones or beans, pounded the victim with a paddle, roasted him by the fire or sweated him limp in steam. If the victim lived, the operation was a success, then as now. You can hear their descendants on the radio any evening telling all the sick to come and be cured. Tecumseh and the Prophet were great sorcerers in Indiana. When old Tetepachsit of Munseetown got too friendly with the whites they accused him of witchcraft and burned him at the stake at Andersontown. Such were the folks our great-grandparents met when they came to Indiana. The long wars since 1689, first between the French and English and later between the English and Americans, had made them hostile to all white people.

About two and a half centuries ago—the dates are not exact—French traders and trappers came to Indiana from Canada. They were unlike the English; they came to trade with and to civilize the natives and then return to their homes in France or Lower Canada, Montreal and Quebec. Most of them had served in the French regular army and all were members of the Canadian militia. In time some of them brought their families and others married Indian girls. After a half-cen-

tury or so, about 1700 to 1730, they had begun
to make homes among the Indians at such villages
as Miamitown, now Fort Wayne, at Weatown,
now Lafayette, and the Piankeshaw village, now
Vincennes. Others lived at palisaded hunting
posts such as Tassinong and Vallonia. They sent
back a fair report of this new land. The soil was
rich, game was abundant and the weather much
better than that of France. Doubtless other
French peasants would have followed and they
would have spread over the land much as the
Americans did a century later; but the French
and Indian War, and Pontiac's War which followed, destroyed all these settlements except
Vincennes, and fear of the British drove half the
settlers of Vincennes across the Mississippi River
into Louisiana. A scant dozen families were left
at Fort Wayne and Weatown and nearly two
hundred at Vincennes. Thus perhaps a thousand
French settlers remained to welcome the Americans and become citizens of Indiana.

The Frenchmen had had military training and
spent their time hunting, in social pastimes, or on
long trips to Montreal or New Orleans. Aside
from its danger such a trip required a half-year
and the *voyageurs* would return with as much
goods as they could carry in their canoes and on
their backs. They took little or no interest in
farming or building and had no ideas of politics,
government or business. All belonged to the
feudal peasant class of the Grand Monarch.
There were not more than a half dozen independ-
ent farmers around Vincennes. These held two
or three hundred acres each and called themselves
Grand Seigneurs of the King. They lived in queer
houses, a kind of cross between a log house and a

palisade. Two rows of poles or small logs were set upright in the ground, about three feet under, and ten feet above ground. The space between the rows, perhaps a foot, was filled with dirt. The tops of the logs were tied together with cross poles for joists and then other poles set up for rafters and all covered with a thatch roof of swamp grass. Around the sides lean-to porches were built. These were their baronial castles. In their baronial halls, the lean-to sheds, the barons held their courts and smoked their long-stemmed clay pipes or sipped their wild-grape wine. On Sunday the Grand Seigneur hitched up his family chariot, a home-made wooden wagon, with solid wooden wheels on wooden axles. The chargers were a pair of scrawny steers, or perhaps a milk cow and a steer. The wagon bed or box was then covered with straw and the junior ladies and lords, decked out in what European clothing and cheap jewelry they could sport, piled in. The squeaking wheels announced to the village folks the start and gradual approach of the high-born family.

The peasants or commoners lived close together in what is now the southern part of the city of Vincennes. Southeast of town they had a large common field in which each villager held two small patches of one or two acres each. In one of these patches he raised wheat and in the other vegetables. Each year these patches were redistributed so that no person held the same strips for two successive years. The field was plowed with wooden plows drawn by oxen. After this the cultivation was done with hoes. If tradition is correct many a brawl in this common field resulted from women and children trampling on other peoples' patches or eating radishes, turnips or melons be-

10

Plow

longing to other people. All of these scraps had to be adjusted by the parish priest who almost alone ruled this little flock. In their little homes the people were very sociable and entertained as lavishly as their limited persimmon beer, wild-grape wine, pies and cakes would allow. A number of these French settlers became prominent in early Indiana and their descendants scattered throughout the state.

As early as 1740 American traders came among the Indians of what is now Indiana. During the Revolution scouting parties from Pittsburg and the Kentucky country visited many parts of the territory. In 1786 some six hundred Kentuckians marched up the Wabash to the sites of Covington and Attica. In 1791 Charles Scott led 750 Kentucky militia from Madison two hundred miles northwest to Lafayette and never saw an Indian until the war on the Wabash. A few months later five hundred more Kentuckians rode from Cincinnati up the eastern border of the state to near Portland, thence across to Logansport, down to Lafayette, and home by the line of the Monon Railroad. Among the frontier people of Kentucky, Virginia, Pennsylvania and the Carolinas, these men spread the report of the beautiful country north of the Ohio.

These frontier folks had not been able to buy land in the older states and were now travelling West to settle and make homes in the new lands west of the mountains. Thousands of families had already crossed the mountains and were living in Kentucky and in the Northwest Territory along the upper Ohio River. As soon as the wars were over—nearly all of the men had been soldiers—they began pushing ahead, and by 1800 were crossing into what is now southern Indiana by thousands. Many of them while they lived in Kentucky had, in parties of four or five, crossed over into Indiana during the autumn weather to hunt and look over the land. In this way quite a few picked out home sites before they moved across the Ohio.

They were a strange people—English, Irish, Scottish or German, yet all American. They had no leaders, no orders, no plan; each acted on whatever knowledge, information or hope he had. They asked little of the government beyond a good title to whatever land they might select for a home.

An Irish lad bargained with a ship-captain to bring him to America. He worked in Virginia five or six years to pay his passage, came West and served as an Indian scout a few years after the Revolution and settled on the banks of White River, one of the first settlers of Gibson County. A couple of boys were captured by the Indians in western Pennsylvania, reared among the Miamis, served for years as scouts and interpreters, ran trading stations at Munseetown and Strawtown and became the founders of Connersville. During the troublous times of the French Revolution a band of Swiss-French refugees—emigrant nobles —came to southern Indiana and built new homes on the banks of the Ohio around Vevay. From the vineyards on the sunny hillsides they made thousands of gallons of wine for the markets of Cincinnati and New Orleans. Thirty or forty miles away a band of canny Scots from Scotland—they had fought for a deposed king—made their homes around a blockhouse which they called Fort Buchanan. A Virginian who had come out with

Clark remained a few years in Kentucky, then moved up on the Little Miami in Ohio, where he founded Xenia. With a neighbor, Robert La Follette, he walked to Vincennes on a land-looking trip. He bought (and sold) the site of the later New Albany, then, attracted by the beautiful location, he bought the land where Madison now stands and founded the town. As one of his first neighbors Mr. Paul had Mr. Lanier, a French Huguenot, who had been driven from his own country for religious reasons. Mr. Lanier was a business man and his son became one of the great men of the state. We still preserve his house as a state monument of our respect. "Purty Old" Tom Montgomery had chased Indians and bears in three states and in his old age brought his family, dogs and horses to the dense woods of Posey County hoping to get a few more shots at his favorite game while his folks opened up a farm. An aristocratic son of a bankrupt planter of Virginia finished his college course at William and Mary, secured an appointment in Wayne's army worth about fifty cents per day, married an aristocratic daughter of a bankrupt land speculator and came to Vincennes to make his home. He and his grandson became presidents of the United States and the state maintains his old home in Vincennes in his memory.

From the same Chesapeake country and bearing the same family name came another college man, to forget his disappointment in love. He became a hermit in the woods north of Madison but later became lieutenant governor and a worthy citizen of Salem. From the distant Yadkin came a better hunter than his older brother, Daniel Boone. After ten or fifteen years of hunting with

13

his brother in Kentucky, Squire Boone located on a little farm near the mouth of Blue River where he could enjoy hunting and escape from the Indians into a nearby cave. From Tennessee came a son of one of the heroes of the long and bloody Cherokee wars. When his neighbor of Corydon was killed at Tippecanoe he took command of the "Yellow Jackets." After four or five more years of Indian fighting he became Indian agent upon the Wabash and finally superintended their removal from the state. On an island in the Wabash at Logansport one may yet visit his beautiful home. Away back in the "Old French War" some Quakers in southern Pennsylvania, rather than have their scalps sold in Philadelphia or Niagara—the Indians found a good market for them at either place—moved down into the Carolinas. Not finding the red sandy soil there to their liking they loaded all their property possible on their high-wheeled wagons and came through Cumberland Gap and by the Wilderness Road to the Ohio at Cincinnati, then up the Whitewater to Wayne County. By the time Indiana became a state there were ten or fifteen thousands of them. They freed their slaves in Carolina but many of the colored people followed their old masters to Indiana. From Kentucky came a young man who had "read" medicine. After serving with the "Rangers" he located in a village among the hills and became the father of the State University. About the same time there came a college man from Princeton University. After learning how to "roll" logs and to use the squirrel rifle he became the first president of the State Seminary. From northern Virginia came a hunter and his wife. After serving with Clark and hunting Indians and other game from his Kentucky home for ten or fifteen years he, his wife, and their children crossed over the Ohio and settled in a small valley girt 'round by overhanging cliffs. The father, mother, and their younger children passed on to Illinois. Then before he died the old hunter "got one more Indian and winged another." His grandson was a scout on the Great Plains and piloted Forty-Niners to San Francisco. Father, son and grandson thus hunted Indians and wild game from Philadelphia to San Francisco.

Just back of Louisville lived Colonel Andrew Polk. While he was out hunting one day, just after the Revolution, the Indians swooped down and carried off his wife and four small children. He succeeded, after three or four years, in getting them all back home safe. They then moved over into Indiana. The oldest son was a scout for Harrison at Tippecanoe and later a member of the first Constitutional Convention. A daughter spent her life as a missionary among the Miami Indians. From their home in Virginia, by way of Ohio, came the Quick family, father, mother and a "passel" of young ones. From Madison a son explored northward along the Indian trails into the wilderness for a hundred miles. At the Hawpatch (Bartholomew County) they opened up a farm and made a famous home.

So this story might be continued about hundreds and thousands of the first Hoosiers. These and such were the folks who first settled Indiana. Eastern historians always refer to them as "poor white trash." The world had not seen their like nor will it again. They were poor. Scarcely one in a hundred had half enough money to pay for

Axe

Pick

Hand Saw

Auger

Plumb Bob

his home. But they were not poorer than those who settled other states. They were likewise white. Many had owned slaves but all freed them, though many of the freed colored people followed or came with their former owners rather than remain in the land of slavery.

They brought very little property—on an average a horse or "critter" for each family. Apparently about half, before 1816, came in wagons and of these latter at least one-half in ox wagons. Of those who came on foot or horseback, the average household property was a quilt or coverlet, a change of clothing, a pot and "spider" or three-legged skillet, an axe, hatchet, two or three steel knives, a hoe and a few other trinkets or trifles. To this outfit the wagoner added a few more tools, a plow, some pewter dishes, a box of valuables—the family "chist"—and some bed clothes. There were no travellers' guides and hence no regularity in the outfit. Each grown man, without fail, carried a rifle and with each family came one or more dogs. Milk cows, pigs, chickens, farm seeds and the like were brought by those who could afford them. Clocks, carpenters' kits and other tools were to be found here and there—one or two in a neighborhood.

There appears no rule in the selection of homes. One located his house near a spring; another, fearing "shakes" and milk sickness in the springs, preferred to dig a well and use the well-known well sweep to lift the water. Some preferred the sandy soil near the larger streams; others preferred the rolling land with loam or limestone soil. Some selected the heavy forest; others preferred the open dales or even prairies. However, there was general objection to the

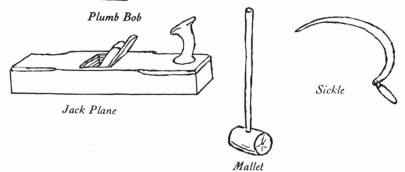

Jack Plane

Sickle

Mallet

prairie. Land that wouldn't grow timber wouldn't be "likely" to produce farm crops.

If a single man (or a family man for that matter) was just moving over from Kentucky or Ohio, he came in the autumn, built a "lean-to" or "half-faced" camp, cleared land during the winter, put in a small crop and late in summer returned and brought a wife or the family. This was the most satisfactory manner. If there were other settlers they would all gather and in a few days a small log cabin would take its place in the community. Some went immediately to work, others took life leisurely, dividing their time between farming and hunting, while still others lingered awhile and passed on. There was always better land just a little further on—"over on Shiney." All started from scratch and the race was on.

Conestoga Wagon

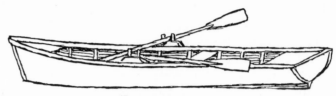

Ferry Boat

A CABIN IN THE CLEARING

Whoopee! Ain't That Somethin'?

A traveller down the Ohio River about the time Indiana became a state would not have seen a single town on the Indiana shore. Had he looked more closely he might have seen small clusters of houses, mostly log, at Lawrenceburg, Vevay, Madison, Jeffersonville and New Albany. At the three last-named places roads from the landing led up through the willows to the town. There was nowhere what we would call a street. Our traveller was not much interested, for he had been told in Pittsburg that there was nobody living on the Indian, or "Indiany," side but a few "hoss thieves" and other criminals who had run away from the older settlements.

Had he known what to look for he might have observed one of the most interesting scenes in our whole history—our folks crossing the Ohio River. All day long and frequently all night, when the river was not too rough, the ferrymen crossed back and forth, ferrying people over into the "promised land." The best ferries used poplar skiffs, twenty feet long, round bottomed, keeled, with sharp prows, double wooden-peg row locks and oars made of linwood or poplar, bought at Pittsburg. They were built to ride the waves, and

18

one scarcely ever swamped if properly handled.
They could ride the waves safely after the big
boats had to tie up when the river was rough.
They could be safely loaded until the stern was
down to within three or four inches of the water
level. They were easily rowed, responding gracefully to oar and keel. Of the vast throng which
crossed, "Old Man River" took a very small toll,
less in twenty years perhaps than the automobiles
take now in one day in our state. The oarsman
made an allowance for the current. If he wished
to land straight across, he usually rowed upstream
half the width of the river and then started across
with bow pointed upstream at an angle with the
current. Then with firm, steady strokes the boat
moved across so that the waves gently parting
from the bow were scarcely noticeable.

It would seem the ferryman's life was monot-
onous, but every crossing had something new; no
two outfits were alike. If it were merely a single
traveller, or a man, his wife and children, toting
all their "earthly possessions" on their backs, the
job was easy. They stepped into the skiff, were
rowed across and disappeared into the great forest to the north. The next load might be a ram-
shackle old wagon drawn by horses, mules or
oxen. Generally the folks and their household
stuffs were taken first. Then the boat returned
for the wagon and live stock. The wagon had to
be taken apart usually and the live stock had to
swim, a line being fastened from the neck of each
to the stern of the boat. Horses and cattle frequently swam loose if there was good landing on
the opposite shore, and once in a while a party
swam their horses across without boats. Few
pioneer women were swimmers, but most of the

men and larger boys could swim a mile or so in the open river, if it were not too cold and rough. Frequently two or more families met at the ferry and often strangers after a long, lonesome trip, met and thus became neighbors for life. Others were close-mouthed and went their ways in silence. The ferryman was always able to tell them of the country beyond as he had heard it from returning travellers. Whatever their experience at the ferry, they had crossed over Jordan into "the sweet fields of Eden." All became vividly interested in the strange land and the possibilties of a new home. Here the new life began. Here they said good-by to the old man, expecting to return, but few ever did. How readable it would now be had the ferryman recorded what they said as he ferried each across, but the page is forever blank, the tongues forever silenced.

Such were the ferries. Those emigrants who came straight north from Cumberland Gap, past Lexington, Kentucky, crossed at Cincinnati or at Aurora down below Lawrenceburg, and joined with the throng who came down the river for the Whitewater Valley, Franklin County, Connersville, Cambridge City and Centerville. Farther west they followed the west bank of the Kentucky, crossing the Ohio at Ash's Ferry, now Lamb. Thence they took the trail for Vernon, Rushville, Columbus and the center part of the state. Those who stuck to the old Wilderness Road by Shelbyville, Kentucky, and those from Boonesboro and Harrodsburg crossed at Gwathmey's Ferry to Jeffersonville, Clarksville and Charlestown, where they took the Traders' Trace to Columbus and later to Indianapolis. Farther down the Ohio a still larger number

crossed at Oatman's old ferry to what is now
New Albany where they took the buffalo path
over the Knobs for Paoli, Hindostan and the
Wabash at Vincennes. Or skirting the eastern
edge of the Knobs to Providence (now Borden)
they went on to Salem, Bono, Palestine (now
Bedford), to Bloomington, Spencer, Greencastle,
Crawfordsville and the Wabash at Lafayette.
This was the ancient hunting trail of the Wea
Indians.

Others from Louisville crossed by Oatman's
new ferry which landed them below the Knobs
where they took the trail for Corydon, Jasper
and Vincennes. This was also an old buffalo trace.
Many who came through Cumberland Gap
turned west from Crab Orchard or Harrodsburg
by Bardstown and Elizabethtown, some crossing
at Brandenburg by Mauck's Ferry to Mauckport
and Corydon, whence they took the Buffalo
Trace, or headed due north to the Wea Trail at
Palmyra, thence to Brownstown and Columbus.
Others from Elizabethtown crossed farther down
the Ohio at Thom's Ferry, better known as Fre-
donia, whence it was only a few miles north to
Pilot Knob and the Buffalo Trace. This trail was
better known at that time as the Governor's
Trace, since it led from Governor Harrison's
farm on Blue River to his home at Vincennes.
Still others bearing farther to the west crossed at
Borer's Ferry, or down where Lincoln crossed at
Tobin's Ferry, both in Perry County.

Those who came through Knoxville over the
Nashville Trace skirted the Cumberland plateau,
turned north and crossed at Yellow Banks to
Rockport. Thence a trail ran north to the center
of the state. In after years many a returning flat-

boatman trudged this weary road north through the Lincoln country, past Dale, Jasper, Shoals, Hindostan, Bedford, Bloomington, Gosport or Martinsville, or if he preferred to spend the money he might ride the stages that ran from Indianapolis to Rockport over the old Rockport road. Just a little below he could ferry at Newburg and take the army trace opened up by General Harmar past Petersburg to either Liverpool (Washington) or Vincennes. Finally there came a vast number from the Nashville country to Red Banks, now Henderson, who crossed to the Evansville-Vincennes road, crossing White River at David Robb's Ferry at Hazelton. Above Vincennes they followed the Piankeshaw hunting trail to Carlisle, Terre Haute, Rockville, Montezuma, Covington and Attica. Such were the main trails by which our folks disappeared up into the great forest land of Indiana.

There were at the time, 1816, about twelve thousand homes in the state, yet a passenger in an airplane ten thousand feet high might not have noticed a single house outside the towns. The region was perhaps as beautiful a forest as the world has ever known. Year after year forest fires had burned away the leaves and underbrush until only the large trees remained, their limbs intermingling and shutting out the sky. Armies on horseback had traveled through it without pretense of cutting a road. Flowers in season grew everywhere. In the open glades were meadows of wild grass and the hill country from New Albany to Greencastle was covered with wild pea vines, acceptable to horses and cattle as our clover. Streams of water rambled here and yonder, apparently content to remain in the deep shades.

A CABIN IN THE CLEARING

When the sky was clear the sunlight trickled through here and there; in storm the great trees groaned and bent before the wind, and the rain dripped from the wet leaves for hours after the cloud had passed. The opened-eyed movers were on the alert, for they were now in Indiana. Occasionally there was a cabin in a clearing and friendly settlers came out to chat with the movers and invite them to spend the night.

They received all kinds of advice. "The soil is purty thin up on the headwaters," they were told at Franklin and Connersville. "Don't go up thar unless you can live on crab apples." "Some fine land up on the Muscatatuck," they were told at Madison, "but don't go up into the hickory land on the flats." At Vernon they were told there were fine locations on Flat Rock but it was a long way from the river. At Salem, "good deep sile up around Vallonia and Brownstown on Driftwood, but it takes a mighty sight of choppin' in them thar woods. If yer want good rollin' land and fine springs go over toward Bono, Palestine or above. They say that limestone land produces somethin' amazin'."

At Petersburg they were told to "stick to the hills" although the oldest settlers over by Maysville and Liverpool declared they "couldn't mind ever seein' or hearin' of anybuddy ailin' or dyin' in that region." At Paoli and Bloomington they were told there was wonderful soil over on Big Shiney but not to go up into the big flat woods. At Indianapolis they were told the squatters up in Boone County had moss on their legs clean above their knees and that all the bullfrogs had died with the shakes above Noblesville. At Vincennes and Carlisle they were warned to be "keerful of speckelaters up and around Tare Holt." So the gossip continued and after every fresh report the little family of movers went into a huddle. The best land was always just a little farther on.

There was no agreement on what was the best site for a home. In some counties as many as one thousand people settled in a single year. Of course all could not have first choice even if each knew exactly what he wanted and all wanted alike. Two families came into the state soon after 1800. One settled near a big spring. There were some small patches of level land, nice sloping hillsides, a clear gravel-bedded stream and, at the time, plenty of game. It was a good home for a good family. The land is still owned in the family and is worth perhaps five dollars an acre and was never worth more. The other family selected a beautiful level tract of rich land, worth now about two hundred dollars per acre. Both families have prospered about equally. Many avoided the springs because they thought the dreadful disease, milk sickness, lurked in the spring branches. Some avoided the low lands because jack-o'-lanterns or will-o'-the-wisps hovered over the wet meadows and wherever the jack-o'-lantern wandered there were the fevers. Whole sections had to be avoided because the deadly nightshade grew there and would kill all the stock and perhaps the children. The limestone soil would "perduce" but it was heavy and sticky. The light or dark sandy loam where the beech, sugar or spicewood grew was better. Many, no doubt, bought land "jinin' " an old friend or relative. Others with visions of wealth located on the large streams whence they could load their flatboats for New Orleans. No explanation will fit all selections. Soil, water, vegetation, drainage, roads, neighbors, hunting, "lay" of land—each had its influence and rarely did two people agree on which was most important. Brothers disagreed and settled miles apart; children when grown up, moved on to different locations; and many families, after a season, packed up and moved farther on.

In many cases the man came alone in the spring, cleared a small field and, while the crop was growing, built a house. Then in the following winter or spring he moved his family to the new home; quite as often he came in the fall and built a house, brought his family in winter or spring and began clearing land for his spring planting.

In any case the first work was a camp to live in until some kind of a house could be built. The "half-faced" camp was common. It was made of poles, usually with three walls, and covered with poles and brush. A bed or beds were made of leaves and grass and woven coverlets or skins were used for covering. A fireplace for warmth and cooking was made outside, usually in front of the open side of the camp. An oven could be made in the hillside with walls of clay or small stones from the creek bed. The common cooking utensils were a spider or three-legged skillet in which to fry meat, and a larger skillet with a lid, in which corn pone could be made. Venison steaks, squirrel and other fresh meats were usually broiled or roasted on spits or sticks. Often in fair weather the outside cooking was continued after the house was finished. Little work was wasted on the camp, if health was good, for the first rush

Cooking Pot

Broom

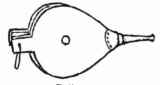

Bellows

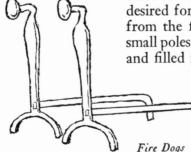

Fire Dogs

was to "get somethin' growin'." If the settlers were in a hurry, and nearly all were the first years, the brush was cleared away and piled in a row at the edge of the field to serve as a fence, after which the corn, potatoes and garden seeds were planted. The new soil was loose and could be plowed or dug up between the rows while the seeds were coming up. Meanwhile the large trees had to be deadened or girdled. This consisted of chopping a notch through the bark and sap entirely around the tree. If a hickory, oak, beech, sugar or poplar the tree would die in a few days; the leaves would wilt and thus allow the sunshine to reach the growing crop.

As soon as the crop was planted, if all went well, the settler proceeded to cut about twenty logs, each about one foot in diameter and perhaps twenty feet long, and an equal number ten, twelve or fifteen feet long. These were for sides and ends of the house. Then came three or four, each shorter than the one below, to form the gables. Each log was notched at the end so the corners would not build up faster than the walls. If the logs were straight and carefully notched each log would rest on the one beneath so neatly that they formed a solid wall. Smaller poles were laid on the top logs to serve as rafters. If two rooms were desired, cross logs could be fitted in at the middle. At side or end three or four logs could be cut to form a door perhaps three feet wide and five feet high. At the other end a hole was made three or four logs high and whatever width was desired for a fireplace. A chimney was built up from the fireplace, formed of a framework of small poles or split sticks a couple of inches square and filled in with clay. The fireplace was lined

26

with stone and then all was heated slowly until it was glazed and fireproof. Some time before winter came, the spaces between the logs were filled with clay and small pieces of split wood. This was called "chinking." If good clay could be had it made the house snug and warm. The roof was made of clapboards split with a frow from some nice straight-grained oak. Each clapboard was about four feet long, six inches wide and an inch thick. These were laid on overlapping and held in place by weight poles. A door was made of split pieces of wood similar to the clapboards and hung on wooden or leather (buckskin) hinges. Finally the floor was made, the first one probably of six or eight inches of clay well packed down and then covered with white sand. Later when a foot adz or broad axe could be had a puncheon floor could be put in and windows added. It took a good workman to build such a house that would keep out wind, rain and snow. Not a nail was used and few of the first settlers had more than an axe and a frow to work with.

By driving a post in the floor and laying poles to the walls a bed was soon made in one corner and in another corner beside the fireplace a table was made. Three-legged stools had to serve for chairs until time could be found to make better ones from hickory poles with woven bark seats and backs. Wooden bowls were burned out, especially if a large sound knot could be found. Years later these utensils would give way to metal or earthenware pots and pans.

Some time before winter a small house was built over the spring. This in time grew into a house for the storage of vegetables, meats, milk and fruits, serving the pioneers as an icehouse or

Frow

Adze

Chair

Broad Axe

refrigerator. A pool of water was provided just large enough for gourd or bucket and not large enough to permit the water to become warm in summer or freeze in winter. Later perhaps a smokehouse would be set up in which to smoke and hang the hams and sidemeat.

As soon as possible an ash-hopper would have been built. First a log, some two feet in diameter, was split. Half of it was hollowed out into a trough, with one end left open. In this clapboards were placed uprights forming a large funnel shaped hopper. As fast as burned, ashes were placed in it, before they were wet, until it was full. Then water was poured in until it stood on the top. When this water leached through, it ran out the open end of the trough into something prepared to hold it. Next it was necessary to get an iron "kittle" to boil the dark lye water and mix it with a proper amount of bear or hog grease to form soft soap. Most probably a kettle could be borrowed somewhere in the neighborhood by walking five or ten miles. It would weigh thirty to sixty pounds and have to be carried home. People could of course make out without soap, but the sweat and grime from the black logs let loose much easier with a small piece of soft soap; and wash day with hard spring water and no soap was not appreciated. However, the small children could never see any use for it.

The soap and lye were also necessary to change the deer hide into buckskin. Thongs of buckskin were always handy when there were no nails or screws and perhaps no augur. The family might all get along "barefooted" until frost came, but it would certainly soon come and then shoepacks and moccasins would be necessary. It would be

Ash Leach

28

several years until there would be a tannery near where folks could have the deer hides tanned or trade them for leather, and they might not live to see ready-made shoes for sale in the country stores. Moreover, pioneer work was hard on clothing and more than one suit of buckskin would be worn out before the spinning wheel could be made and flax and wool grown and spun for linsey-woolsey. Most likely first settlers would not live to buy a ready-made suit of clothes or dress.

The planting season was the most important of the whole year. The settler had to raise his "grub." What he didn't raise or kill he did without. He might borrow from or "swap" with a neighbor but there was no grocery. The first season settlers had to depend largely on themselves. Friendly families along the road might give them a few seeds and tell them something of farming in the new home, but most of it was a great experiment. Corn and potatoes were necessary and fortunately anyone could raise them. Cornbread, meat and potatoes would do, but they got to be common, three times a day through the long winter and spring. The garden belonged to the women and on it depended the table, the one great attraction of pioneer life. Long, hard work in the outdoors developed enormous appetites for men, women, children and dogs.

The first warm days in March a brush pile was burned and in the mingled soil and ashes the cabbage, tobacco and pepper seeds were sown. The tender plants were covered to protect them from frost. As soon as all danger of frost was over and "the sign got in the head" they were transplanted or "set out" in the garden. There were early

Winnigstadt cabbages for summer use and big "Drumheads" for fall and winter. (A pot of "biled" cabbage with a chunk of fat meat for "seasonin' " is mighty "fillin' " when everybody is "dog tired" and "hog hungry." Besides, for every drop of "Dutch" blood in your veins, there must be made a gallon of sauerkraut.) Equally "pushin' " were the lettuce and radishes. By the middle of April a row or two of each would be in the ground. After the first year a bed of potato onions would be planted in the fall and covered with straw or fodder to prevent heaving out of the ground. These sturdy fellows came early and led in time all the garden truck. If the appetite was too strong, greens and wild onions could be found and nobody turned up his nose at a ham bone "biled" in sour dock or polk. Some early "bunch" or "pole" beans and perhaps some garlic made up the summer garden. All these with new potatoes, peas and roastin' ears were supposed to be on the table by harvest time—many of them earlier. Folks had to wait until wheat could be threshed and flour ground before the big juicy berry cobblers could be added to this early summer menu.

With the corn planted and the early vegetables coming on, gardeners turned to the winter vegetables. Far the most important were the potatoes and beans. After the potatoes were grown they could be left in the ground until after the hot weather, then dug and piled in a cool place and with the approach of winter "holed up." As soon as the corn was up three or four inches high the field-beans could be planted—one or two "cut-shorts" or "navys" beside each hill of corn. If these were planted too early they would climb

all over the corn and pull the stalks down, ruin-
ing the corn. The beans grew rank and a few
short rows would produce a bushel or two of
hulled beans. Not only that, the "cutshorts"
bloomed all fall, and fresh tender green beans for
cooking could be found here long after the garden beans were gone. Bread was the staff of life,
all right, but a pot of boiled beans and a hunk of
hog had restoring grace after a long hunt in winter or a day of hard chopping in the "new
ground." The farmer didn't like to be bothered
with the beans in his corn but there just had to be
dry beans in the house from January until June to
"bile" with the pork. Potatoes gave out in February usually, and nothing was left but the corn
pone, pork and beans to make up the bulk of his
grub.

Ten or twelve hills of cucumbers had to be
planted somewhere. They didn't care where.
Give them a start any place and they would cover
up everything else with their thrifty vines. No
respectable people would eat them for they
caused "summer complaint," "chills," "biles,"
"yaller janders" and maybe cancer and consumption. But the housewife usually sliced three or
four of the fat, chubby "cukes" with an equal
amount of onions or lettuce and covered it over
with vinegar and somehow it disappeared from
the table. But their principal use was for "pick-
ling." Some time during the fall if possible the
settler made a barrel or tub and filled it with vinegar or brine. Into this the wife placed two or
three bushels of the fat young cucumbers and
petrified them for winter and spring use. A half
or quarter of one of these fossils, so sour they
would wrinkle one's face just to look at them,

made an excellent relish with corn pone, hominy, beans or fat pork. In the cornfield also the pumpkins were raised. Usually planted, one seed in each corn hill, about the first of June, they would begin to vine about the time the corn was "laid by." They were no trouble to raise and in the absence of orchard fruit "punkin" butter made a good side dish for fresh meat. Cut into thin strips they could be hung in the top of the house to dry and so kept all winter.

If there were any children it was necessary to plant about one hundred hills of popcorn. Some time toward the last of October, the little ears were gathered, strung and hung on the wall to season. On winter evenings it was good sport to sprinkle the grains in the hot embers of the fireplace and then catch the fluffy grains as they hopped out.

Sage and red pepper were also needed where there was so much fresh meat to be cooked. In the neighborhood some place a few slips of sage could be obtained. These were set out in the garden and grew into dwarf bushes two feet high. In the fall when the velvety leaves were full they were picked and dried and put away to keep dry. A half dozen leaves crushed fine and sprinkled over the frying meat gave it a flavor which is still relished and the little sage bushes still keep their places in our gardens.

Pepper seeds were planted in a box, usually, and when two inches high transplanted to the garden. One could nearly always borrow a dozen plants from a neighbor. They grew about a foot high and each plant produced ten or twelve red pods the size of hen eggs. When ripe they were picked and laid away like the sage in a dry

place. One or two pods in a pot of beans or cabbage would "cut" the grease. Peppers were also
considered healthful, especially in the hot summer and fall weather when dysentery, chills and
typhoid fever were common. The old folks will
remember strings of red peppers hung in grace-
ful folds on the walls.

Finally, about the first of June, a small patch
of new ground was prepared and the turnip seed
sown. Turnips were best when about the size of
duck eggs. The larger ones were hollow or pithy.
Most of them were eaten raw in the fall and winter, before apples could be had. Two or three
bushels were "holed up" like the potatoes for
spring cooking. They were generally boiled with
pork. Occasionally a garden would contain a row
of parsnips. These were shaped like radishes and
grew likes radishes, but were "holed up" and
cooked in the spring like turnips. A "patch" of
watermelons, and they grew almost without attention, in the rich weedless soil of the new
country, filled up the circle of farm and garden
crops. Occasionally there was a field of hemp and
nearly every farmer had his field or "patch" of
tobacco and flax, but they were not for food.

The log cabin with its clay chinking, its rude
doors and windows and mud and stick chimney,
was not a thing of beauty. It remained for the
wife to make it into the log cabin of poetry.
Walks of flat stones were laid to the spring, to the
garden, to the barn and to the road, if one were
close. On either side of the walks, beds of flowers
were planted. Hollyhocks of all colors, wild
roses, marigolds, verbenas, bachelor buttons and
whatever else could be borrowed, begged, or
traded for among the neighbors, together with

33

Well Sweep

plants that could be transplanted from the forest, kept one's eye from the unsightly logs. A trellis of poles supported the honeysuckle (trumpet) vine that transformed the door into a bower. Gourd seeds planted at each corner not only helped to decorate but the fruits were extremely useful. Jonah's gourd was no miracle to the early settler. Almost overnight its vines covered the walls and dozens of long-handled calabashes hung down like huge ear bobs. Scores of these ripened gourds cut in all forms were used as dippers, cups, saucers, glasses, cans, boxes and ornaments. If everything else failed the morning glory came up of its own accord and covered everything with its luxuriant vines. Like all things common and lowly it was not appreciated, but there are few things in the flower world more beautiful than a riot of filmy, velvety red, white and blue morning glories. Under the spell of the flowers the cabin-in-the-clearing changed from an unsightly pile of poles and mud to a dream of beauty.

The work was not done when the crops were grown. These pioneers never lived to see—maybe even hear of—a seed store. So as things ripened seeds had to be gathered and carefully stored away. This was where the little gourds came in handy. Each with its particular "batch" of seed, free from mice and insects, was hung on the wall or fastened to the rafters. Most of the crops matured in one season, but Messrs. Turnip, Parsnip and Cabbage had to be kept green during the winter to produce seed the second year. This again was woman's business. She always tried to gather more seeds than she would need so she could swap with some neighbor for a new variety. Also some neighbor's cabin might burn or a new

Gourd Dipper

Gourd Container

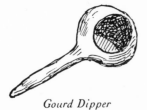

Gourd Dipper

34

"mover" might come in, needing help. "Seed swappin'" was a social pastime among pioneer women in February and March, somewhat as bridge is now. While they were "swapping" seeds they also swapped methods of cultivation. Some had "best luck" one way, some another, but all kept eyes on the sun and moon and planted or transplanted when the "sign" was right. The famous proverbs or "sayings" of Franklin come from such talk among the German farmers of Pennsylvania. The descendants of these same "Pennsylvania Dutch" were by far the best farmers in early Indiana.

While gathering seeds for next year's sowing the prudent housewife also laid in a supply of medicinal "yarbs." Mullein, polk-root, calomel, mint or hoarhound could be obtained at any time. But senna, pennyroyal, elder blossoms, and many others had to be gathered in season. The habit or custom persisted, and even today in many homes bunches of these may be seen in the attic carefully put away against the time when colds, sore throat, rheumatism or indigestion put in their unwelcome appearance. Such, in brief, were those first eager years of pioneer life in Indiana.

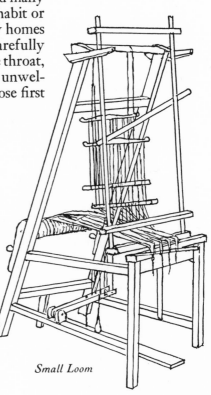

Small Loom

35

Stage Coach

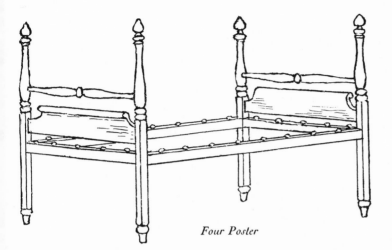

Four Poster

THE INDIANA HOME

When the settlers of Indiana decided to organize a state it was necessary for them to have a state home. They asked the United States government for nearly the same boundaries as the Indiana Territory then (1815) had. They thought it would be better if they had a lake front on Lake Michigan, and Congress added a ten-mile strip across the north end of the territory. In the language of the Act of Congress, April 19, 1816, the new state was bounded on the east by the meridian which forms the western boundary of Ohio, which is the meridian of the mouth of the great Miami; on the south by the River Ohio from the Great Miami to the Wabash; on the west by a line along the middle of the Wabash to the point where the meridian of Vincennes last touches the west bank of the Wabash, thence north by this

37

meridian until it intersects an east and west line drawn ten miles north of the south tip of Lake Michigan; on the north by a parallel ten miles north of the south tip of Lake Michigan. This is the legal description of the boundaries as you see them on the map. Three of the corners are in the water. The new state (modern surveys show the land area to be over 23,000,000 acres) contained 21,637,760 acres, enough for about 135,000 farms of 160 acres each.

Brace and Bit

Inside these boundaries were all kinds of lands and soils. The north half of the state was a vast level plain covered, except in the west, with a heavy growth of hardwood trees. This forest varied somewhat from south to north. Oak, walnut and hickory were common throughout the state, but the sugar maple, beech and tulips which were so plentiful in the south were scarce in the north. Sycamores were common along the streams throughout the state, their white trunks and stately branches rivaling the oak and tulip in size, marking the water courses. They stood up like aristocrats among the other trees and, like aristocrats, they were useless to man and beast. They produced no fruit and their bodies could not be used for lumber, rails or firewood. Squirrels and raccoons avoided them on account of their treacherous bark. Occasionally a pair of eagles built their home in the tall branches. Though rarely ever sound of body, with dead tops or dead limbs, one rarely ever saw a totally dead sycamore. If the farmer cut it down the stump refused to die and was soon covered with luxuriant sprouts. Some of the sycamores grew to a diameter of seven feet, although not usually as tall as the tulips and hickories.

38

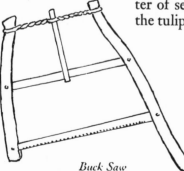

Buck Saw

The most stately of the forest trees was the tulip, the poplar of that day. It usually stood, like Saul in Israel, head and shoulders above the multitude. It spread its long arms in benediction over the heads of the humbler trees. It grew in all soils but best in the sandy loam of a deep cove protected from the wind. It was a favorite with the settler. The slender poplar trunks were used to build his first cabin, while the larger or middle-sized were used for his more pretentious double hewed-log house. I have seen the hewed poplars from such a house sound after a century of use. A poplar log, or perhaps a walnut, was split into thin slabs and dressed smooth with the adz for the cabin builder's puncheon floor. From the tall straight sixty-footers were hewed the gunwales for his flatboat. After the coming of the sawmill his frame house from sleeper to collar beam, weatherboarded and ceiled, was made from yellow poplar. In the pasture-lot it was the prince of shade trees, tall and symmetrical, as it still is in our parks, yet it had no appeal to the youngsters. It bore no fruit, like the hickory and walnut, and its blasted top limbs showed that it rather held kinship with the lightning and storm. The old sycamore in its hollow trunk offered a nesting-place for chickens, ducks and geese or perhaps a snug bed for the old sow and her numerous family of pigs, or a convenient playhouse for the small children, but the poplar was generally sound. From its upper branches the squirrel could chatter his defiance safe from everything but the experienced marksman with the old family rifle.

Commonest of the forest trees were the oaks—white, red, black, chestnut and chinquapin. They flourished everywhere, even in the sandy bot-

Sledge Hammer

Tomper

Shovel

toms and swamps. They were sturdy, straight-grained, sound and strong, the most perfect representatives in the forest of the pioneer folk. From them were split the rails that enclosed the fields; from them were riven the clapboards that covered the buildings and the tall palings that encircled the house and garden; from them came the woodwork of the wagons and plows—hardest and strongest of the straight-grained timber. In later years the pioneers hunted out the chestnut oaks, not numerous like the white oaks, and got the bark for their tanning vats. No use was made of the timber, and the long slender naked bodies were left in the forest to rot. Before the neighborhood tanneries disappeared the chestnut oak was a stranger in our forest. The ebony acorns of the chinquapin were almost equal in flavor to the chestnut, and the children found it worth while to gather a few gallons and lay them away for winter use. If the supply ran short the boys could usually find more by cutting a beech snag and robbing the storehouse of the readheaded woodpecker. The white and red oak also bore vast crops of acorns which, when they fell in autumn, covered the ground, but they were bitter. Under the name "mast" they furnished ample food for the half-wild and wilder hogs through the long winter. Thousands of squirrels, not to mention "bre'r coon" and bruin, lived on the abundant supply of acorns. The failure of the acorn and beechnut crop in southern Indiana before the Civil War was almost as great a calamity as the failure of the corn crop.

The heavy demand on the oak timber came from the shippers. Apples and apple-jack, corn meal and corn whiskey, pork and flour—each and

all went to market in barrels made from oak
staves. Late in the autumn after the farmwork
was done, the men went to the woods with crosscut saw, axes, mauls and wedges and made the
staves, each about three feet long and an inch
thick, "without knot, crook or wormhole."
These were built up into four-cornered stacks,
fifty to the stack, and left to season or dry. Next
came the coopers with their shaving horses and
drawing knives—"draw-shavers"—who dressed
them down to even thickness, tapering at the ends
and so well-matched that barrels for whiskey and
brandy and curing meat would be water-tight.

Oak was the only timber of the whole forest
that would hold brine and whiskey, in fact the
only container in all creation that would hold the
latter. The tattoo of the coopers' hammers as they
tightened the hickory hoops on these barrels
could be heard in every neighborhood. At Madison, at the opening of the pork season, about the
first of December, one might have seen five acres
of barrels piled three on end, thousands of them.
Even today as one travels along the Wabash from
Logansport to Huntington, or in the northern
part of Clark County, one sees large holes or pits
in the ground where lime was burned. Flatboat
loads of lime packed in oaken barrels or casks
were shipped yearly to New Orleans for the
cholera-infected country down South.

When the railroad builders came in the Forties
and Fifties and sought a reliable support for their
iron rails, they selected the oak crosstie, generally
made of small-sized trees one to two feet in diameter. It took a half million of these to lay the first
Monon tracks alone. Yet all this little more than

Cooper's Horse

marked the great forest. The slaughter came in the Seventies and Eighties when the oil companies began the use of oak barrels for shipping kerosene. I have seen 5,000,000 white oak staves stacked at one landing on the Ohio River ready for shipment to Cincinnati and Pittsburg. We are told that our farmer pioneers wasted our forests. Such is not the truth any more than that the Indians destroyed the wild game.

No trees of the forest were quite so attractive to the boy as the hickory. In the spring he watched with feverish interest as the hickories clothed themselves in their fluffy catkin flowers, nor was interest lessened until the little hickory nuts began to peep from under the big drooping leaves. An untimely frost might kill the flowers but nothing untoward could happen after the hickory nuts were as big as peas. The season was sure to be a success. The apple tree and even the peach had some more or less relation to work, but the hickory nut tree was pure enjoyment. On the high ridges and along the rocky hillsides the shell-bark or shagbark grew, while along the streams or in the sandy bottoms were the big hickory-nut trees and pecans. The shellbarks grew so tall and the bark was so rough that the barefoot boy— even as tough as Whittier's—would hesitate to climb a tree to shake the nuts down. If they could not be reached by throwing a club, one just had to wait till wind and rain shattered them down and take his chances with the squirrels, for of all the food in the forests squirrels were fondest of the small thin-shelled hickory nut. On the other hand many of the trees bearing the large nuts had wide low-branching tops, among which the boys could climb and thresh down the whole crop at one time, often a bushel or so of shelled nuts. The mellow autumn weather, the gorgeous decorations of the trees, the last appearance of the song birds, all combined to make this a carnival of nature for the country children. There were no rich or poor, all had an equal chance. The walnut and hazelnut contributed in a way to the winter supply but the hickory nuts were the first prize.

For general usefulness the hickory timber did not rank so high as oak and poplar. It was stronger than oak but would not endure the weather. It was used for the axletrees of the pioneer's wagon and for the spokes and felloes of his carriage—when he got one away down in the "glorious Fifties." Axe handles were made exclusively of the white wood of the hickory, as were the mauls used in splitting rails. The long slender fingers of the grain cradles were usually hickory, though ash and mulberry were often used. Nor must we forget that bows and arrows, those deadly weapons of the younger boys, were generally made of well-seasoned hickory.

However, the greatest commercial use for hickory was as hoop-poles. It required judgment, skill and strength to cut these products. It was a certain proof that the boy had become a man when he could take his dinner bucket and hatchet and go into the big woods, select the slender hickories, six or ten feet long, one inch in diameter at the top, trim them and tie them with hickory withes into straight bundles of ten or twenty, and set them up so they looked like an Indian tepee. The smaller ones about six feet long were used for hoops on the ordinary produce barrels, the longer or hogshead-size for the larger barrels. Flatboat loads of these went to New Orleans

43

where they were used on the cypress barrels for sugar and syrup. A good "hand" would cut eight hundred per day. So many of those poles came from southern Indiana that hoop-pole and Hoosier were almost synonyms of the region.

We must not forget also that the Democrats used the tall slender hickories for flag poles in honor of "Old Hickory." These poles were frequently one hundred feet high and by the Fifties often carried a rooster at the top. The Whigs and later the Republicans used poplar. Every village had one or more of these "election" poles. Hickory was preferred for firewood and an arm load of hickory bark produced quick results on a cold morning. Those with highly developed taste smoked their pork and even venison hams with hickory bark; but the bark gave off so little smoke that the more common practice was to store the smoked hams in carefully collected ashes of hickory bark. Hickory hams, however, were so good that far more were sold than were ever delivered. You can still buy "country cured" and "hickory" hams on the Chicago market!

Closely associated with the hickory was the walnut. The latter was well distributed over the entire nation. While the nuts were not so highly appreciated they were quite as widely used. Any youngster between the ages of seven and fourteen who didn't have his hands stained a rich dark brown in October was considered sub-normal. The hulls themselves were widely used in coloring yarn, although the bark of the tree was as frequently used. The nuts were so plentiful, a single tree sometimes producing eight or ten bushels, that many of them lay on the ground for squirrels and hogs after the hickory nuts and acorns were gone. Walnut timber was not much used by the early settlers. Occasionally a tree was split into fence rails but for this purpose it did not compete with the oak, and it was totally out-classed by poplar in house-building. Not until the Forties and Fifties when travelling cabinet-makers, mostly Germans, came to Indiana, did the walnut timber come into its own. After being sawed and seasoned for a year or two it took on a finish not surpassed by anything but mahogany, and only equalled by the wild cherry and hard maple. The old four-posters, wardrobes, bureaus, hautboys, "chists," and whatnots built by these cunning craftsmen, fitted together without nail or screw, still show the dazzling beauty of our ancient walnut timber. Close kin to the black walnut was the white walnut or butternut, now remembered mostly for its use in coloring yarn the standard gray or butternut of the old time homespun. The timber was of a lighter color and not so capable of polish as the black walnut. Occasionally one sees today in southern Indiana, a corner cupboard of white walnut, now more than a century old.

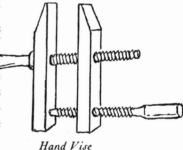

Hand Vise

The beech trees were the most clannish of the forest. Sometimes a park of five or ten acres was fully occupied by beeches. They grew close together and carried a heavy foliage. Perhaps the dense shade helped to kill out the other timber. Grass rarely grew under them as under most other forest trees. They bore enormous crops of small three-sided nuts, sweeter even than the shellbark or hazelnut, but so tedious to pick the kernels from that they were left to "bre'r coon," the squirrels and hogs. In fact the hogs preferred beechnuts to any other food to be found in the forest. In years of heavy beech mast, old razorback hogs became so fat that the meat all fried away into grease, and so lazy that those intended for the market had to be put in training before they marched away to Cincinnati or Madison, and the old sows became so fat they neglected to raise any pigs. Beech woods were a paradise for the squirrel. Almost every tree had a hollow snag or limb in which the squirrels could hide from the hunter, store their food and make their homes. The limbs of the trees interlaced so that the squirrels could jump from branch to branch and need scarcely ever come to the ground.

The beech groves generally indicated light fertile soil and the timber was easily cleared. If the trees were girdled while in full leaf they died quickly and rarely sent up any sprouts. In about two years the limbs began to fall and then on some dry day fire would do the rest. Excepting a prairie fire in the Kankakee marshes, there was nothing more spectacular than a fire in the "beech deadenin'" with a score or so of hollow trees spouting fire fifty feet from the ground.

The hard maple, the sugar tree of the pioneers, was closely associated with the domestic life of the first settlers. It was a noble tree, ranging in size up to four feet in diameter and eighty feet in height. Maples frequently grew in groves of one hundred or more on a few acres. They indicated good soil, and unlike in the beech grove, grass usually covered the ground. The first warm days of spring, called a "thaw," usually in February or March, sent the sap upwards to waken the buds for their summer work. During the winter the settler had, or at least should have, prepared small wooden troughs, holding about one gallon each, from the little poplars. As soon as the sap began to run, he cut a V-shaped notch, angle down, in the sugar tree and at the lower point of the notch inserted a spout made from a joint of the alder bush, or from cane if obtainable. The sap trickled from this spout into the trough and the work of sugar making was on. There was little other work at this season of the year to interfere and everybody—men, women, children and neighbors—resorted to the sugar camp. As large an iron kettle as obtainable, sometimes one holding forty gallons, was arranged so that a steady fire could be kept under it. The unmarried folks volunteered to keep the fire burning throughout the night. The weather was frosty and the camp fire enjoyable. Everybody was hungry for something sweet. As the "sugar water" slowly boiled down the syrup or "sugar molasses" was drained off. Further boiling would produce maple sugar, often poured hot into little moulds shaped like hearts, shamrocks or pies. Thus the work or play went on until all were fed up and as much more prepared as could be taken care of. It was the first relief from the long winter and the introduction to Spring and the great "outdoors."

Along with the sugar tree must be mentioned the sassafras. Not that they were kin, for lowly sassafras had no kin, but merely that in the life of the pioneer they were thrown together and supplemented each other. If the lordly poplar represented the aristocrats and the sturdy oak the strong middle working class, the humble sassafras represented the poor. Like them it was found wherever it could get a scant foothold. It was no match for the forest trees, which easily crowded it out. It rarely grew to be more than six inches in diameter and thirty feet high; more often one

inch through and six feet high. If it found an un-
occupied spot it multiplied, like the poor, so fast
that all were stunted and almost starved to death.
After being housed up during the long winter
and eating heavily of corn bread and pork or
venison the settler's blood was so thick and slug-
gish in the spring that he was "full of humors,"
lazy, and might have "biles" (boils), so he took
his hoe and laid in some sassafras roots from which
he made tea, sweetened it with sugar molasses,
and drank liberally. Soon his blood was sparkling
through his veins like the rills from the melting
snows, and he was "fit" for the arduous struggle
with nature which he called making a crop.

Still worse, due to exposure in rain and snow or
sleeping in the attic or shivering over a smoky fire,
he may have got "rumatics"—the "jint-water"
may have dried up in his "jints" (joints)—or have
got a "crick" in his back. In each and all cases he
boiled the sassafras bark until the liquid would
burn the skin like fire, rubbed it on and dried it in
until all symptoms disappeared. You will still find
the extract of this lowly spicy wood on the drug-
gist's shelves, either under a classical title or most
probably in a pretentious bottle dedicated to Saint
Jacob.

If the pioneer were a little fastidious and objected to the democracy of sassafras tea he could
in some shady, sandy nook, especially in the
beech and sugar groves, find bunches of spicewood, a dark-complexioned shrub four to eight
feet high, whose small branches placed in the tea
kettle made a sufficient substitute for store tea.
Like sassafras it thinned the blood, was sweetened
with maple sugar and was to be drunk only in the
early spring. Anyone drinking either of these

teas in the autumn would so thin his blood that he
was certain to freeze to death the following winter—at least we were told so. Sassafras and spice
teas bore about the same social relations among
the pioneers that "coke" and champagne do
among us.

In the fruit line nature offered quite a menu.
Earliest in the spring came the service, pro-
nounced "sarvis" by the pioneers; it is the modern
shadbush, Juneberry or amelanchier. It was a
shrub six to fifteen feet high, growing on southern hillsides. Its blossoms, appearing before the
forest leaves, covered it as with a white robe and
seen at a distance against the somber color of the
leafless woods, looked like a lingering patch of
snow. There were a dozen or so within a mile of
our house, all known and numbered. The little
round berries, the size of peas, reddened in May
and had to be attended to strictly or the birds and
squirrels looted the whole crop. Two hearty
youngsters could take care of the output of a
whole tree at one feeding—perhaps a half-gallon.
Occasionally some unnatural impulse would lead
us to gather them in our hats and take them home
for a cobbler. They tasted much like the cherry
and too many had the same disastrous effects on
the teeth. Did you ever have your teeth "sharp"
or "on edge"? If not, just thank goodness and go
ahead with your reading.

Following the "sarvis" came mulberry time.
Here again was a nice social distinction. The "sarvis" was for the alert and enterprising. The big
juicy squashy mulberry was for the proletariat.
The trees sometimes grew to three feet in diameter though rarely more than twenty feet high.
The low huge horizontal limbs of such a veteran

49

might extend out from the body of the tree a greater distance than the total height of the tree. Onto these limbs the youngsters would climb and sit as in a hammock and eat and eat. Some finicky persons objected to the bugs but the bugs, too, were full of mulberries and made no difference to the taste. It was coming-out time for young squirrels, and, not having previously been killed, they frequently came into the same tree with the boys. Both liked mulberries but their conduct differed. The squirrels ate a half-dozen berries or so and turned it into a frolic; the boys usually ate a gallon, reluctantly climbed down and resigned themselves to two hours of exquisite bellyache. Jim Crow was fond of mulberries and perhaps he ate them for the bugs.

The service and mulberry merely introduced the berry season—in fact they were not popularly classed as berries at all. On the sunny slopes of southern Indiana a century ago the wild strawberry grew in plenty. An early traveller remarked that his horse's hoofs were red with their juice. Even at that they had no place in the household economy of the pioneer. They ripened toward the end of May and were picked by the youngsters between the ages of five and twenty, as were the service and mulberries. They were easily transplanted and many a pioneer garden had a bed large enough to supply the local or family demand. A century was to pass before they became a marketable product.

The king of the tribe was the blackberry. It grew freely in all parts of the state wherever a small unshaded spot gave it a place to start. Even after careless farmers had worn the soil from the hillsides, gashed with gullies, the blackberry bush and the sassafras were nature's first aids in restoring vegetation. The largest Indian village in the state, Kekionga (Fort Wayne), was in the midst of the most extensive brier patch in the state. The name itself refers to the abundance of the berries. They grew in open patches in the forest, they grew on the roadside, in the meadow, in the fence corners, in the graveyards, and at the doorstep; and wherever they grew they brought forth their fruit abundantly in season. Fortunately they ripened about the beginning of the harvest season before many of the garden vegetables were ready for use and at a time when the menu was reduced practically to bread and meat. The housewife built them into one- and two-story cobblers, into round pies for dessert and the four o'clock harvest lunch, and finally she preserved as many as possible in the form of jelly, jam, and marmalade. Canning was not begun until about the Civil War period.

In the northern part of the state, especially in Noble County, were large huckleberry swamps but they were not used much by white people until the middle of the century. Raspberries grew in all parts of the state but were not so plentiful. They preferred a shady nook where the soil was largely black sand. Though tedious to pick they were the tastiest of all the berries. Nothing on the pioneer table excelled in taste the dark-red wild raspberries, fresh from the vine. The prudent mother usually put up several bottles of raspberry cordial to tide the babies over weaning time or to use as bracers for Granny after she reached the allotted three-score-and-ten.

Earlier by a week or two was the dewberry. It grew on the open, sunny hillsides—preferably in worn-out fields. The vines ran on the ground like watermelons and were quite as long. The berries were coarse-grained and not so well flavored as the raspberry but, coming earlier, they filled a long-felt want on the dinner table. When dewberry pie was passed the youngsters laid aside knife and fork if they had them, and each seized a quarter section in both hands and ate it as one would a slice of watermelon. After the encounter his face and front were usually covered with the red evidence of the combat.

Berrying, however, was different from nutting. The berries were for table or family use, which changed the whole occupation from play to work. The youngster was not seriously hurt if he were left at home when the gang went to pick berries, but when they went nutting he simply wasn't left. The thorny briers scratched bare ankles until they were raw. Where the briers couldn't get the chiggers could. There were four hundred ways to keep chiggers off, or to get rid of them if they got on—and they always did—all useless. There was no more exasperating pleasure known than scratching chiggers and it is still done, contrary to the best medical advice. Besides, the berry patch, especially a raspberry patch, was the best harbor in the forest for black snakes. Anywhere from two- to five-foot long varmints lay quietly among the vines, either watching for birds or eating berries, I never knew which. They were not backward for a scrap. The women were usually in a panic, for somebody had heard that one sometime, somewhere, had wrapped himself around somebody's neck and if somebody had not pulled him loose somebody would certainly have been choked. Nevertheless a ten-year-old boy always accepted the challenge. Generally by the time the snake was organized for the fight, his body gracefully coiled, his head a foot in the air, and his red tongue dancing, the dog had reinforced the boy and the battle was soon over. A thousand years of instinct taught Towser never to rush a coiled snake, but the instant it broke coil there was a quick rush, a vicious snap and shake, and Mr. Blacksnake or Racer was a limp wreck. It only remained to drag the snake out into the sunshine to see if he would turn his white belly up to the sun. If he did, he wouldn't die until sunset, or it was going to rain or something else.

In the fruit line autumn brought the pawpaw, persimmon and crab apple. None of these was of any great value yet all were widely distributed over the state. On the headwaters of the Whitewater were hundreds of acres of crab apple trees —dwarf, scraggy trees, three to six inches in diameter and as high as the peach. In the early spring they were an ocean of white blossoms, alive with wild bees. The apples, about as large as hickory nuts, ripened in September and October. They were, even when ripe, so hard and sour the wild hogs avoided them. By dropping them in boiling water the peel and core were loosened. These removed, there remained about two bites of apple. This by the addition of a liberal amount of sugar or molasses could be made into preserves, which was decidedly better than nothing, its only competitor. Men would drive twenty miles to get a wagonload of these crab apples for winter use.

The persimmon was more common but was usually left unmolested for the humorous opossum. Sometimes they (the persimmons) would hang on the small trees until a light freeze took the pucker out of them, when they could be eaten with less reserve. The old French settlers around Vincennes made barrels of beer from them but the practice never took among the American settlers. A good persimmon pudding, however, was not to be sneezed at. The pawpaw grew on a small tree, rarely over ten feet high, but generally clean-bodied, straight and, if out in the open, very symmetrical. The fruit was from the size of a hen's egg up to a big fat cucumber, and when ripe a golden yellow. It was a dainty with many pioneers and the taste still lingers. If gathered carefully and laid away in a cool dry place pawpaws would keep a month or so. Though of no comparative value they offered a pleasant variation before the apple orchards appeared. With some persons they produced hives, provided they ate as many as two dozens at a time. Like the persimmon they were especially revered by the opossum family.

Finally, one must not omit the wild grape, the fall and fox grape—in some communities known as the October and winter grape. The fall variety were about as large as peas, the fox about the size of buckshot. Grapes were common throughout the state. Though they frequently climbed sixty or eighty feet, they flourished best on a smaller tree ten to twenty feet high. The vine was ordinarily one to two inches in diameter though I have seen fox grape vines six inches in diameter and running ninety feet high. One could usually find plenty of fruit in reach from the ground but it was not uncommon to cut a tree for grapes. The fall grape had a flavor not excelled by any cultivated grape and so far surpassed the winter variety that the latter were left to foxes, raccoons, pheasants and the brown bears. Bunches hung on the stem for a long time, the former until frosts had dropped all the leaves, the latter until Christmas or later. The thrifty housewife usually gathered several gallons and put them up in a stone jar if such could be had, covering them with a syrup of some kind, honey or New Orleans molasses most frequently. The wild grape was also a favorite with the fall hunters who often went deep into the forest and built their shacks. Grapes were relished as a variety to their meat diet.

As widely distributed as the grape was the wild plum. It grew as a dwarf tree rarely higher than ten feet but it was rather clannish, often forming almost impenetrable thickets of an acre or more. One could be detected a mile away by its mass of white blossoms, rivaling the crab apple and the hawthorn in beauty, a treasure house for the wild honeybees. The fruit, a size smaller than the crab apple and a rich yellow in color, ripened in October. It was so tart that even yet nothing has been discovered or invented sweet enough to sweeten it. Nevertheless, it had a pleasant taste and would beguile the fruit-hungry youngsters several miles as a bait. It was made into a marmalade or plum butter for table use. The farmer usually left a few plum trees along the fence row for home consumption. The plum was a prolific bearer and seldom failed of a crop.

Red and black haws (hawthorns), the former the size of large cherries, the latter half as large, and not so tart or sour as the plum and crab apple, offered further variety to these forest fruits and complete the tale of the forest tree menu.

Though not of such general interest to the

whole pioneer family as the forest store of fruits, of far greater value was the store of game. The great majority of first settlers went in debt for their land. On an average it was five years before the farm itself was yielding a surplus. In the meantime payments at the government land office fell due. From the commercial or economic standpoint, the deer led the list. Of the total number in the state in 1816 one can only guess—probably more than a million. They were frequently seen in herds too numerous to be counted. Beginning about 1790 it was common for Kentucky hunters to cross into Indiana around the last of October and establish hunting camps back several miles from the Ohio. The hunters usually returned home after a month's hunt with six or eight pack horses laden with deer and bearskin and meat.

As early as 1733 it was estimated by the founder of Vincennes that 30,000 deerskins per year were shipped from that post. If he was correct then at least 100,000 were shipped from what is now Indiana, for Ouiatenon and Fort Wayne were each more important trading posts than Vincennes at that time. United States soldiers at Forts Knox, Harrison, Wayne and Steuben in Indiana were regularly furnished with rations of venison. Captain Leonard Helm, an officer under George Rogers Clark, furnished the garrison at Fort Nelson (Louisville) from about 1782 to 1800 with venison killed on the north side of the Ohio. Flatboats carried loads of venison hams and hides to New Orleans from 1790 to 1820. A number of settlers, including the author's great-grandfather, loaded a considerable part of a flatboat from Perry County as late as 1819 with venison hams and deerskins.

THE INDIANA HOME

A single hunter in Morgan County as late as 1820 killed one hundred deer during the season. In the early days of Johnson County they were so numerous that they destroyed fields of corn. Cured venison hams sold at Vincennes at twenty-five cents each, often twenty-five cents for a pair. Venison was as common on the settlers' tables as pork. The dried hides sold for about one dollar each. Buckskin, with all its imperfections, was the commonest kind of leather. Gloves, shoes, pants, shirts and suspenders—all were made of either dressed or tanned deerskin. While dry it was serviceable and fairly comfortable, but when wet it absorbed moisture like a sponge. Dry moccasins were ideal for the hunter but when wet they were impossible. In snow the wearer often stuffed grass inside his moccasins to keep his feet warm. Around the house the women and children wore them with pleasure.

There were many ways of "hunting the red deer" but the sportsman's way of the English gentleman was not one of them. The pioneers hunted for a living and as in all other occupations their work was cunning rather than scientific. In my own family—my great-great-grandfather hunted deer and Indians for a half-century in six or more states, my great-grandfather for forty years in Kentucky and Indiana—the usual method was horseback with hounds to do the chasing. This required a well-trained horse. There is in our family a tradition of a sorrel mare who, at a word, would stand like a statue while her rider fired and loaded his heavy rifle. Most of the hunting by the pioneers, however, was done on foot. The deer would rarely run far from its feeding grounds and the hunter would lie in ambush at the crossing while the hounds brought the deer around.

The hounds were, in the hunting season, an unsightly pack of bones, covered with a scraggy, battle-scarred skin, ornamented with a long tail and two mangled flaps which once had been ears. They were tireless and bloodthirsty. They tackled a bear or panther with the same eagerness as a deer and stayed for the funeral, often their own, if an old bear or panther was in the fight. Everyone knew his neighbor's dog and, if a good citizen (either or both), respected it. An indignity to a deer hound brought swift and often bloody defense from its owner. The hound was inoffensive and rarely even noticed a person entering the house. A cur usually guarded the premises and watched over the children. Unless a prowling panther or wildcat came near the hound passed the summer months in indolence and poverty, getting what satisfaction he could from life in his struggle with flies and fleas.

Many successful hunters stalked their game at early dawn or twilight while the deer were feeding, or ambushed them on their trails—probably near a salt spring or "lick." Or they quietly paddled along the streams with a brilliant torch, shooting the astonished deer as he gazed in wonder at the strange sight. This latter procedure was called shining their eyes—a method still employed in killing bullfrogs. After the hunter killed a deer or bear he stopped only long enough to bleed the dead animal, gut it, if the weather was not cold, and hang it up beyond the reach of the dogs and wolves. A panther was usually too shy to go about such a place. When the hunt was over someone returned with pack horse or sled and took care of the carcass. Fawns were rarely killed except for table use or for a "baby blanket." What the beaver was to the fur trader, the deer was to the first settlers.

Bears were more readily found and killed than deer. They frequently lived in hollow trees. These were well marked and the bears easily killed. The dogs would chase one up a tree, usually within a mile of discovery, and all the hunter had to do was to come up and shoot it, using some care to kill it, as a wounded bear might injure or even kill a good dog. A fat bear had several gallons of grease which served for lard in cooking. His skin, if not sold, was used for a robe or for bed clothing. Bears had an ungovernable appetite for young pigs and generally got themselves killed in an effort to rob the settler's pig pen. A settler would kill all in his neighborhood in a year or so. The "painter" (panther) was more of a liability than an asset to the settler. Frequently he would badly frighten women and children along the forest paths, for he had a habit of following along overhead in the trees; at night his cries were blood-curdling to hear. If one were known to be in the neighborhood, the deer hounds were put on the trail and followed by two or three skillful hunters. When the big cat was treed the hunters approached cautiously, hoping for a dead shot. His pelt made the most beautiful robe or rug in the pioneer home.

The buffaloes were gone from Indiana before many American settlers arrived. In 1764 when George Croghan was in Indiana there were vast herds of them. There is a tradition that during a cold winter, about 1800, heavy sleet covered the ground for nearly three months during which most of the buffaloes starved. Those which did not starve fell an easy prey to the hungry wolves. At any rate they disappeared quite suddenly about that time. Most probably hide-hunters were to blame, for these animals were easily killed and their skins were valuable.

In the lakes and swamps of northern Indiana there were beavers in considerable numbers until about 1840, but they were trapped by men, red and white, who made that a business. Beaver trapping was not a side line for the settlers and farmers as deer hunting was.

There was an endless abundance of lesser game —squirrels, rabbits, raccoons, opossums, pigeons, ducks, quail. Hunting these was no serious business for grown men, but Towser and the boys recognized no season on any of them. The squirrels were a pest in the southern half of the state and destroyed thousands of bushels of corn annually. In general one did not have to go off his own land to kill all he needed. They were as common on the dinner table between 1830 and 1860 as venison was before 1820. Wherever in the state there was timber there were squirrels, and the more they were killed apparently the more plentiful they became, at least until the heavy forests were cut in the Eighties. Stories of marksmanship with the small-bore squirrel rifle were as plentiful as fish stories at present—and about as airy. A squirrel hunter didn't qualify until he had killed at least thirty in a couple of hours without wasting a shot.

Of all the animals in the great forest the raccoon was the most cunning. He was a fisherman by trade and so long as he stayed close to the streams and was satisfied with crayfish he was

safe. But he had an irresistible longing for roasting ears. The first dark, drizzly night after the
roasting ears were in season Mother Coon and
her family of three or four glossy half-grown
coons would set out for the cornfield. Towser
was easily awakened by the racket and the boys
were soon in the chase. The coon family were
pretty lucky if one or more skins were not tacked
up to dry next day on the barn door. Later in the
autumn and in early winter when the fur was
prime the younger men joined in the sport. The
movie of today is no more attractive than was the
coon hunt then, to break the monotony of long
evenings. Mr. Coon wore a glossy fur coat worth
about fifty cents, but the scrap with the dogs furnished a dollar's worth of entertainment. If the
stories are true the old-time coon dog grew mar-
velously wise.

The opossum seems to have been created for
the boys to hunt. He couldn't have been made
uglier or clumsier. Any excuse of a dog could
chase him up his beloved persimmon tree and any
live boy could climb up and shake him out or pull
him down by his long slick tail which he let hang
down conveniently for that purpose. He was well
known for his habit of playing dead or "playing
possum" when attacked. His coat of fur was
worth only ten or fifteen cents and few persons at
that time would eat him, but the small boys lugged
him home in triumph nevertheless.

Rabbits were seldom shot in pioneer days;
rather they were chopped or twisted out of hollow logs or trees, caught in snares or run down in
the deep snow. They were considered best when
caught in the deep snow and the meat allowed to
freeze a day or two.

61

Of feathered game, the wild turkeys in the south and the ducks in the north were most important. While not as common as pioneer stories would indicate there were many fine turkeys in Indiana a century and a quarter ago. Their favorite pasture grounds were the beech woods. It was next to impossible to see them in the woods while the leaves were on and they were very wary at all times. From December to February they were fat and that was the customary time for hunting them. Sometimes when surprised, perhaps by a dog, they flew up into a near-by tree where they could be stalked, especially if they were busy watching the dog. Another way of hunting them was to find their roosting place and wait until daylight. They roosted in the trees and did not fly down until after daylight. A full-grown gobbler weighed from twelve to fifteen pounds and led the list of meats for taste.

The northern lakes and swamps were literally full of ducks, geese, brant and teal in season and thousands were there at all times. The settlers had them on their tables in and out of season. But the fall and early winter, when the nesting season was over and before the larger number had started south, was the most common time for hunting them. They could be hunted again when they returned in the early spring or dropped down for a few days' visit in their long flight from Florida to Canada. One can only form an idea now of their abundance by seeing them in flocks of tens of thousands on their southern feeding grounds in January and February. The easiest way for the hunter to get these water fowl was to hide in the high grass near the edge of the lake and wait until they came near. A favorite weapon was the old smooth-bore Queen Bess or Harper's Ferry musket, loaded with buckshot or slugs. If the hunter was not himself killed by the kick of the musket he could usually pick up five or ten ducks after each explosion. However the pioneers killed only what they needed and made no impression on the numbers of ducks and geese in the immense flocks. Not until after the Civil War, when market hunters and that species of mankind which kills wild animals for sport, came with breechloading shotguns, were they destroyed.

Prairie hens were not nearly so numerous and had little chance before the high-powered breechloaders or magazine guns. Quail shooting was not practical until a comparatively recent date, but the small boys in the early days often trapped the quail in boxes set on trigger and baited with corn. In certain seasons when there was a heavy mast (beechnuts and acorns) the woods were full of wild pigeons, about the size of quail. At times one could visit their roosting place at night and with a torch and club kill a sackful, but their coming and going were so uncertain that little dependence could be placed on them for food. At times they literally darkened the skies for hours with their passage. With the passing of the great forest they disappeared completely. Not a living specimen of the passenger pigeon can be found anywhere today.

In the whole world it would be difficult to find a tract of land the size of Indiana better provided with streams and lakes. Scarcely one of its ninety-two counties but had a flatboat stream, and many of the streams were large enough to run a pioneer gristmill. The general course of its streams is southwest. Although the state borders for twenty-five miles on Lake Michigan only eight or ten counties drain into the Great Lakes. While not accustomed to navigation the early settlers soon learned to construct from the forest trees rude boats, load them with produce and navigate them to New Orleans. The Wabash and its tributaries furnished downstream transportation to fifty counties, and small steamers regularly plied its waters until the railroads made such transportation unnecessary. While we have no actual count it seems safe to say that one thousand flatboats left Indiana for New Orleans every year. Not more than one-third of these were loaded on the Ohio. Lawrence County alone in the heart of the hill country sent around forty each year, and Morgan nearly as many.

The waters of the lakes and streams contained about all the fish they could support. The ubiquitous catfish was wherever there was water. The ten-year-old boy caught him four inches long in the brook while the old fisherman caught him—maybe—in the Ohio and Wabash weighing one hundred pounds. All the fishing tackle, except the barbed hook, was made at home. Hungry fish would bite anything from a fish worm to liver—crickets, grasshoppers, locusts, caterpillars, lizards, or young mice. All these were plentiful in the new country. In fact "fish bait" was the zero value for everything. Even some men were so "ornery" they wouldn't make good "fish bait." The black bass lurked everywhere, ready to surprise the dozing fisherman or to run away with the small boy's hook and send him home to tell the old story of the "whopper" that broke his line.

The modern sportsman with his reel and rod

64

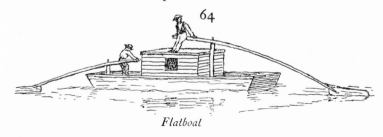

Flatboat

had not appeared. It was "catch as catch can." No sport was more exhilarating to young men from fourteen to fifty than gigging by torchlight. In early spring—late April or early May, according to the season—when the fish were playing on the gravelly riffles, armed with a flaming torch and a gig—a pitchfork or spade would do—wading, knee- or waist-deep in the cold water, one could get real excitement and plenty of fish—especially of fat, sleek, bony white suckers, with now and then a free ride on the back of a four-foot red horse, pike or sturgeon. What a time for the ten- or twelve-year-old boy who went along on the express promise to his mother that he would stay out of the cold water—and he did until he got to the creek, when he promptly but accidentally fell in—clear up to his knees!

Fish was a standard dish on the table but fishing remained a sport. Energetic, hard-working men were not supposed to go fishing. Somehow it was associated with small boys and lazy men. What was dimly in their minds no doubt was the solemn truth that fishing is done by deep-thinking philosophers, not by scientists or artists. Such in brief was the patrimony of our Hoosier home, and such the appeal of its mysterious woods and waters.

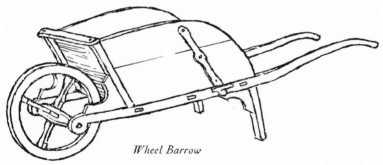

Wheel Barrow

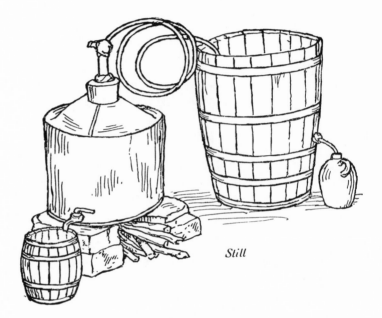

Still

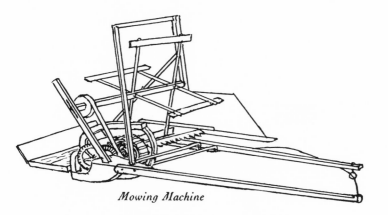

Mowing Machine

FARM LIFE IN THE FIFTIES

In 1800 Indiana, as described in the first chapter was a beautiful wilderness. Fifty years later one million people called themselves Hoosiers. Much less than one-third of the land was cleared. There were probably 100,000 farms and somewhat over 200 villages, towns and cities. The largest of these—New Albany, Indianapolis and Madison—were little more than thickly populated neighborhoods. New Albany and Madison enjoyed a considerable river trade, running up to several thousand dollars' worth in a year. Each of these cities boasted one graveled street, the National Road in Indianapolis, the Michigan Road in Madison and the Vincennes Pike in New Albany. Other streets were mere dirt roads, ankle deep in mud or dust as the weather varied.

The county seat towns like Bedford, Anderson, Elkhart, and Princeton were built around the courthouse squares. The courthouse was usually a square, two-story red brick with the county offices downstairs and the courtroom up. Speci-

67

mens of these are still standing at Corydon, Rome, Leavenworth and Paoli; the latter is a most beautiful building and is still in use. Stores, blacksmith shops, taverns and other public houses faced the courthouse. A hitch rack for the convenience of the farmers encircled the square. On hot days this gave not only the appearance but the odor of a livery stable. Millions of house flies were attracted by the sweaty horses and oxen. The continuous stamping of the animals soon produced a ditch. After a rain it stood full of foul water and when dry held an equal amount of dust. If there was a breeze the dust mixed with manure was generously distributed in the houses and stores across the street; and in the good old days before screen doors, the flies gathered as regularly at the tavern tables for meals as did the other boarders.

The villages were of two general classes. One grew up at the crossroads around a blacksmith shop, a country store and post office. The church and schoolhouses were added later. Four or five families, too poor to own farms but not too poor to raise large families, made up the population. The other village grew up around the gristmill. If the miller had a good dam site with plenty of water power he ran day and night the year 'round. He usually added a store and shop to his mill and made it a business center. Hamer's Mill, now preserved in Spring Mill State Park, is the best example we have left. The railroads put these mills out of business and the villages soon disappeared.

A large proportion of the houses, even in the towns and cities, were log, though brick and frame were appearing. Few of these houses remain outside of the river towns. The farmers generally pitied the poor people who had to live in the cities and towns. Each family in town usually kept a milk cow. In the summer time these cows in droves of five to ten roamed the countryside in search of pasturage. As the pasturage became short in the summer they became skillful in pushing down or jumping over the farmers' fences, causing endless anxiety and bickering. Each family also kept two or three pigs in the back part of the lot to eat up the slop and garbage. But a pigsty, especially in wet sultry summer weather, was not a thing of beauty. Each family also kept a flock of chickens and a garden. For six months in the year the chickens made ceaseless war on the gardens and while not quite so serious as the Civil War which followed, it caused even more neighborhood strife. One of the dark questions which still remains unsolved is why a person's chickens never did scratch up his own garden.

While the villagers and townfolks were thus struggling to make their squalid dirty little towns more attractive, farm life in Indiana was becoming more enjoyable than ever before or since. The central idea in this system was the home and the home was a farm. Ever since our folks had turned away from the seacoast, before the Revolution, they had been clearing farms and building houses in the great forest. The great men whom they read about in American history were associated with equally well-known homes: Washington and Mount Vernon, Jefferson and Monticello, Jackson and the Hermitage, Clay and Ashland, Harrison and Grouseland. The plantation owners in the South were building palaces to equal those they read about in story books. The "Old Kentucky Home" at Bardstown was only one of hundreds of such in Kentucky. One of the sights on the trip to New Orleans was the beautiful plantation houses along the Mississippi from Memphis to Natchez. Some of these, even along the Ohio, built before the Civil War, may still be seen.

To the early settlers of Indiana these houses were only a dream. They had to wait until they had earned a great deal of money before such houses could be built. They had no way to earn money except by their own labor and for that reason many had crossed the Ohio River to get out of the land of slavery. In a hundred years they had developed great skill in clearing the land and making it into farms. Racially they were about equally divided among Germans (Pennsylvania Dutch), English and Scotch-Irish. The Germans had been peasants in the beautiful Rhinelands until their homes and gardens were destroyed by war. The kind Queen Anne sent some of them to America where they found homes in Pennsylvania and New York.

They were a stout, rugged people, who ate heartily and could turn out a great amount of work in the twelve or fifteen hours which they called a working day. If they had time they cleared their fields "smack-smooth," that is, grubbed the stumps and removed the rocks. Their barns were large and usually full of stock and feed; they always had plenty to eat and some to sell, though they bought little. Though they ate and drank voraciously, they seldom touched "hard likker." In the fall they filled their houses and cellars with food, not to mention what was "holed up" in the garden. Huge quantities of apples, cider, cheese, butter, sauerkraut, preserved foods and pork products disappeared over their tables during the winter. They took little interest in books but attended their little churches regularly. They were hospitable to their neighbors and to strangers but ignorant of politics and the outside world generally.

Their daily work, their "in-comings and out-goings," were all regulated by rules based on centuries of observation. Instead of becoming scientific they had become superstitious. They did much of their planting according to the phases of the moon and the signs of the zodiac. Potatoes and other vegetables which grow in the ground were planted in the dark of the moon lest they all go to tops. Melons were planted when the "sign was in the head." Other crops had to be planted on a certain day. Hens and geese were set when the sign was right and a colt born on an unlucky day would never make a dependable work horse. The heavy corn shuck meant a cold winter. If the hogs were restless, "growled" after they went to bed, there would be a change in the weather and the farmer prepared for it immediately. Everything from the chattering bluejay to the clouds in the sky had meaning and was intended by a kindly Providence to direct him in his work. If he failed to see or neglected to heed the warning it was the work of Satan. So speaks the "Dutch" blood in our veins—strong, industrious, plodding and safe.

More numerous were the English. Some of these were younger sons from the Virginia and Carolina plantations. They were a more intelligent group. Most of them were farmers; some were storekeepers, some built flatboats and traded to New Orleans, others became lawyers and politicians or speculators. In general they were the most enterprising and controlled the new society. Close kin to these and coming with them were a poorer class, known in colonial times as redemptioners or indentured servants.

Some of these became successful farmers or business men in the new West but many remained poor and relatively thriftless—half hunter, half farmer. They were masters of the axe and rifle. A small number of full blood Irish and a somewhat larger number of Scots and a few French refugees finished the pioneer band. The Irish were often teachers, the Scots liked to preach and our first great banker was a Frenchman. Here and there was a "college man" from the East. He soon learned to use an axe and rifle, though he practiced law or preached for a living. These people and their ancestors had been in this western forest about a century. The sturdy English were best at clearing land, building houses and mills, the "Dutch" were best at farming while the uproarious Scots, Irish and Scotch-Irish were great preachers, orators and politicians and perhaps had the best time—if they lived long enough.

We can find plenty to read about the heroes of this hundred years' struggle with the wilderness. We enjoy the stories about Daniel Boone, Simon Kenton, Lewis Weitzell, George Rogers Clark, and William Henry Harrison, but not one of them was able to make a real home for himself in the big woods. Between 1750 and 1850 more than a million farm homes were opened up. In 1750 wolves, foxes, bears and deer furnished food to a few straggling, starving, savage Indians. By 1850 four or five million reliant folks had built houses for themselves, of whom one million were in Indiana. If all the property of all the heroes mentioned above, with Lincoln, and Wayne added, had been put together it would not have equalled a good quarter section Indiana farm. In our eagerness to build expensive shrines and monuments to these more spectacular figures we sometimes forget to give sufficient attention to the men and women who made Indiana.

The early farmers worked "the year 'round." The work varied with the seasons but there was no idle season for either men or women. The usual day's work for a man began at sunup and ended at sundown—"from sun to sun." The women worked a few hours longer, since there was wool to pick, socks and stockings to knit and clothes to mend, and these were after-supper jobs. We fret our lives away now for fear some "youth" who weighs one hundred fifty pounds will be compelled by some hard-hearted taskmaster to do a few hours' work. In those days a boy of thirteen or fourteen hitched his team—oxen, horses or mules—to a wagon or plow and did a "man's" day's work. Nor were the girls idle. The gospel of work was taught in church and school and practiced in the home. The Devil was always at the elbow of idlers, for the Devil had plenty of work for idle hands to do. Hard work and sanctity were closely akin but idleness and sin were twins.

The year's work began with the new year. Until Christmas the farmer was finishing up, but with New Year's he faced about and began the new year. The steady work for January, February and March was clearing new land and cleaning up the "new-ground," that is, the field that had been cultivated only one year. Almost every farmer added a few acres, from two to ten, to his plow land every year. If it was not needed by the

73

farmer himself, a wedding was always to be expected and the new couple would need a little extra crop land immediately. Every parent desired his children to "settle down" on adjoining land and while they were getting a start it would be convenient to cultivate a field or two of the home farm on "sheers."

As mentioned above, there was a general plan of the year's work common to all farmers, but no two did their work alike. Some cleared the ground all at one time and put it in corn; others extended the clearing over two years, cutting and piling the underbrush and deadening the larger trees the first year and then preparing it for the plow the second year. The field which was undergoing this process was generally referred to as the "deadnin'." Some farmers cut the underbrush and burned it, others used mattocks and cut out all the big roots near the surface. The latter method made the first year's cultivation much easier. After a year or two the smaller roots would be cut or broken by the plow. The German preferred the mattock while the other settlers depended entirely upon the axe. Clearing was not considered hard or unpleasant work, for it took one into the woods and they were always fascinating. If the day was cold a fire was started and the brush piled on. A roaring fire was always near if hands or feet got cold.

Besides the timber there were on the hillsides of southern Indiana many loose, flat stones. With a low sled and a yoke of oxen these were escorted to the edge of the fields and built into a fence, such as you may still see on the farms of Monroe, Lawrence and Washington counties. Other stones were used for protecting the washed banks of creeks or building roads on the farms. And

while we are speaking of oxen we must not forget that the year's supply of firewood usually
came from the clearing. The trees suitable for
wood were felled, carefully trimmed and left ly-
ing on the ground. The tall, slender hickories,
five to twelve inches in diameter, were best for
this purpose, but dead and seasoned trees of other
hardwoods were also saved for cookstove or kin-
dling. Some day when the snow lay on the
ground, the oxen were hitched to the heavy
"bob" or "log" sled and vast quantities of wood
could be "snaked" up to the wood lot where it
could be chopped up and corded at leisure. This
"snaking" in the snow was midway between
work and play. By the middle of April the clearing should have been finished except for the logs.

Logrolling was almost a trade or an art among
our folks a century ago. One of the chief causes
of the popularity of Governor Jonathan Jen-
nings, our first governor, was his skill at logrolling.
It is said that he would often make a two or three
weeks' tour, horseback, upstate from his Corydon home and help at a logrolling every day. He
enjoyed eating and drinking and both were done
at logrollings—besides, it was the best place to
electioneer. The story is that he would ride up,
hitch his horse and represent himself as a new settler "jist over the way." Then gradually, while all
were "guessing" about him, someone would remember that he looked just like the governor,
and at dinner he would make a short speech. A
governor in buckskin with "both hands on the
handspike" couldn't help but be popular. There
was always someone present who was going to
another "rollin' " the next day and so the governor would proceed. It was a pleasant custom.
Sixty years later Blue Jeans Williams, our great

pioneer farmer governor, was likewise a great
hand at the "rollin's" and there is a picture somewhere of him at one, just one of the boys at the
spike.

The hands gathered early, for it was usually a
long, hard day. The number varied of course
with the size of the clearing. Four or five men for
each acre of the clearing made a good crew. Since
every hand meant a day's work in return, there
was no sense in having too many, but a man was
considered stingy who had too few. The hands
were divided into squads of eight and the battle
was on. Skill and sense were both necessary in
building log heaps. A well-built heap would burn
up without attention; a poorly built heap would
have to be "chunked" from one to a dozen times
—maybe go out a few times. A sensible heap was
one built of the proper timber. Sycamore and
gum wouldn't burn in Satan's big furnace so they
had to be mixed with hickory, beech or dead timber. Each squad had a captain and he was chief
architect for the heaps. A heap that wouldn't burn
was called a "cropper" and two or three "crop-
pers" would ruin a captain's reputation as a roller.

A feature of the rolling was the dinner. When
the hands were invited the last word was, "Be
sure, now, and bring the old woman with you."
Some of the women were famous for their pies,
others for their cakes. Each woman brought some
articles of table service, and all looked forward to
a great dinner. And they were seldom disap-
pointed. Enough girls attended to wait tables and
wash the dishes. Some formality was appearing
and there was generally a "deacon" present to say
grace. It was not uncommon for some wag to
bawl out: "Cut her short, deacon, you know how
hungry I am," or for some snappy matron to

warn: "Save all that prayin' stuff for meetin',
Uncle Hiram, when we have plenty of time; the
vittles are gettin' cold." Being too early for house-
flies there was nothing to mar the enjoyment of
the meal. There was wit and sensible conversa-
tion and logrollers had real appetites.

In the parlor there was a quilt in the frames for
the old grannies with their clay pipes. Deft fingers
directed the needles and defter tongues rehearsed
the gossip of the winter, for this was the first time
these old folks had been out since Christmas.
They were fairly thirsting for a chance to spread
these "I hearns." After the dinner dishes were
washed, the girls and young wives paid a visit to
the clearing to see the men work. When the work
was finished the remainder of the day, if any, was
spent visiting, after which folks set out for home,
most of them to meet next day at another "rollin' " and so on for two or three weeks.

Sometime before the corn was planted a fence
had to be built around the clearing. These fences
were of the Virginia rail or worm type. Each rail
was about four inches thick (square or triangu-
lar) and ten feet long, split from oak, walnut or
poplar. Usually the rails could be made so near
the line of the fence that hauling with oxen and
sled was not necessary. The rails were best made
in the winter while the sap was down because the
timber split better then and the rails lasted longer.
In making the rails an axe, an iron wedge or two,
a maul and at least two dogwood gluts were necessary. The maul was made of second-growth
white hickory. The sapling, five or six inches in
diameter, was cut just below the first roots and a
section one foot long left to form the head of the
maul. The rest of the small log was then dressed
down to the proper size for a handle, the maul

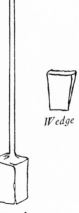

Wedge

Maul

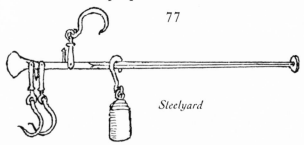

Steelyard

head rounded off and the finished article set in the chimney corner to season.

The gluts were made of dogwood saplings three inches through, each glut being from twelve to fifteen inches long and properly tapered so that it would not bounce. The iron wedge was perhaps shorter than the glut, forged and tempered with precision by the local blacksmith. The iron wedge was used for starting the split, the gluts along its length to finish it. Rail-splitting was one of the more strenuous activities of pioneer farming. Any chap past the age of eight or ten could chop some with an axe but the fellow who could open up a butt cut of a tough four-foot white oak log with maul and iron wedges was a man and no mistake. A good chopper could cut his timber and make perhaps one hundred fifty rails per day. After the crosscut saw came into use, rail-makers working in pairs could turn out four hundred to five hundred per pair of workmen. Much depended on the timber, the tools and the skill of the workmen.

There remained only the job of breaking the new ground. This was done by folks from the South with a jumping shovel plow. This implement consisted of an ordinary two-horse shovel plow with an upright cutting bar or cutter passing down from the beam so that the point of the cutter was a half-inch lower than the point of the plow and immediately in front. The cutter was set slanting slightly to the rear so that it would cut small roots and jump the plow over others. The handles of the plow unfortunately were not wide enough for the plowman to walk between as they are now on the ordinary breaking plow. When the point of the cutter struck a root it

78

jerked the handles down violently. If a handle caught the unwary plowman in the short ribs, it laid him out. If he were walking back out of the way but gripping the handles too tightly, it all but broke his neck. The jerk was equally irksome to a spirited team. In other words a quick-tempered plowman and a fidgety team had little business plowing in the new ground. The ideal outfit was a "philosophical" plowman and a yoke of heavy, patient oxen.

The above description applies in general until about 1840. After that period the farmers frequently used the "deadening" or "woodpasture" plan. In the former the underbrush was cut but not piled, the trees—except the rail and saw timber—deadened and left for one or two years when the torch was applied. As stated in another chapter a beech "deadenin' " on fire was a sight for tired eyes. By 1850 large flocks of sheep were appearing. These had to be kept under fence. If the underbrush were cut and burned and the wood fenced, the sheep would kill the sprouts and thus save the farmer an immense amount of work. However managed, new ground was the outstanding feature of our pioneer agriculture.

Clearing new ground was not all that was going on in the early spring around the farm home of the Forties and Fifties. All nature was waking up and the farmer was a part of it. This period was the heyday of the homespun era and the lambs led the parade of new life in the spring. The flax fields and linsey-woolsey days were passing. The census of 1860 showed 215,375 sheep on the sunny hillsides of southern Indiana. The young lambs, more than one for each man, woman and child, began to appear in February. The little wowsly, wobbly, helpless things might come on a warm sunny day or they might come in a howling snowstorm at midnight. Whenever they decided to come the farmer had to be prepared with a warm, snug place for them, preferably an open shed with fodder set around to break the wind. Much as they liked the warmth, the sheep also liked the free open air. On cold mornings the farmer would often come from the barn with one or two young lambs in his arms, to be guests at the fireside for awhile and to drink warm milk from a spoon until they got their feet again. Many of the lambs were twins and occasionally one was black as a raven. The "black sheep" of the family was not so good but the black lamb of the flock was a pet. The sheep were the most friendly and least dangerous—except Father Ram—of the farm animals, and for a month or two in the spring every child in the family claimed a pet lamb as his own.

Just about the time the lambs got old enough to be frisky—around the middle of May—the old sheep were ready for the barber. The business of a sheep is to raise wool, and as soon as the weather got warm enough in the spring all were gathered in a closed pen, and one by one placed on a table about waist high and clipped. The sheep complained about it much as a five-year-old boy does in the barber's chair, but after it was over he felt better. A good shearer, with a couple of boys to catch and hold the sheep, would clip anywhere from twenty to thirty fleeces per day. A good "sheep barber" took pride in making a nice even cut but some of them left the sheep looking like a freshman's head used to after a college scrap. In the old country the sheep were

Sheep Shears

washed before they were shorn but so far as I know this was not done in Indiana. Washing the wool was done in the earlier period by the women and children. When it came to be strictly a man's job a machine was invented to do it. After shearing, the sheep were turned out on pasture and if sheep-killing dogs let them alone they required little further attention until winter. By the eighteen-forties farmers were taking great interest in their flocks and the little dark Merinos and Cotswolds were being displaced by the larger Spanish Merinos and English Southdowns. One of the oldest of farmers' jokes comes from this time. Governor Joseph A. Wright, although a lawyer, took great interest in the farmers. After addressing a farmers' meeting someone asked him what kind of ram he would recommend. He replied that not being a farmer himself he could not speak from experience, but he had heard the hydraulic ram spoken of very favorably.

We have disposed of the sheep but the wool is still on hand. From here the women and children took complete charge. First the wool was taken to the creek and washed until the grease was all or nearly all out. It was then spread on the clean gravel or grass to dry. After this it was placed in a clean room and picked. This was a tedious job, especially if there were burrs. Slowly it was picked apart and all the dirt taken out. This was an "odd" job for everybody on rainy days and after supper for two or three months, unless there was some special hurry. Between 1850 and 1860 the number of sheep in Indiana increased more than a million. Half or more of the wool, after it was picked, was baled up and sent east over the new railroads. The proceeds were about the first spending money the wife had ever had. Every-body was building a new house in the "glorious Fifties" and Madam could now buy a carpet, a cookstove, a new silk dress, or hire a cabinet-mak-er to come and furnish the new house with that beautiful furniture we now prize so highly.

The remaining half of the wool crop was for home use and formed a more serious problem. By the close of this era, say 1860, there was a woolen mill in almost every county to which one might take the wool and get woven cloth in return, or one might have only the carding done. "Industri-ous" or "thrifty" folks didn't do this but saved it all for homework. First the wool was carded into long fluffy rolls. The cards with which this was done somewhat resembled a pair of fine-toothed curry combs. The rolls had to be uniform in size or else the yarn would not be. After the carding came the spinning—day and night, year in and year out one heard the hum of the spinning wheel, symbol of industry, the poetic charm of pioneer life and slow, sure death to the weary wife. After the spinning, the yarn was colored either with indigo or some one of a dozen barks or combination of barks, run off on the reel into skeins or hanks, or wound into balls as Priscilla

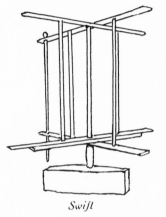

Swift

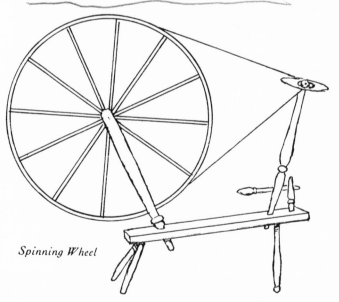

Spinning Wheel

did from the hands of John Alden, and then
turned over to the knitters and weavers. For plain
weaving there was a loom in almost every house;
for coverlets or Sunday dress goods, there was
usually a professional weaver in the neighborhood—most likely a maiden of discreet age and no
cares. Knitting was a pastime. No industrious
woman wasted her time knitting until she became
a grandmother about the age of forty — except
after supper or while visiting. It was good form
for women to invite a friend to "bring your knit-
tin' and stay all day." Knitting was an ornament
to grandmother and she was rarely seen without
her needles in her hand and a ball of yarn in her
lap—unless of course she was darning or quilting.

Every farm likewise had a flock of geese and
these were, like the sheep, under the jurisdiction
of the women and children. A new farmer, just
moving in, might be excused for a year or two if
he slept on shucks or straw, but after that he was
expected to have feather-beds or be classed as "ornery." Most folks used them only to sleep on but
among the Germans the children, who likely
slept in the attic or lean-to bedrooms, slept between feather beds. The ordinary flock of geese
consisted of twenty or thirty, depending on the

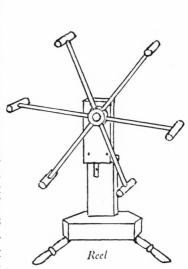

Reel

Flax Wheel

size of the family. Each child when married was given one or two new feather beds.

Like the sheep, the geese began work early in spring. They "stole their nests out," probably around a straw stack, haystack, or by a stump in the fence corner or brier patch. Unlike their barnyard relations, the hens, they never cackled when they laid, but quietly and secretly covered the egg or eggs and slipped away. It was necessary to hunt goose eggs regularly, for a belated snow or frost would chill them so they wouldn't hatch. This was usually a pleasant chore for the children after school. Each goose laid from ten to a dozen eggs and then went on a sitdown strike. She could then be placed in a coop prepared for her near the house, her eggs restored to her and in due time she appeared with a family of fluffy little helpless goslings. Mr. Gander in the meantime stood quietly and patiently on guard. With the appearance of the goslings, like all proud fathers, he at once assumed all honor and responsibility and led the family off to the creek. Geese could be picked or plucked three or four times a year and perhaps each goose would produce a pound of feathers annually. They were beautiful birds when in full feather but like anyone else, I suppose, a proud gander felt humiliated after he was plucked—much as a sheep after he was fleeced.

Geese had the worst reputation for downright meanness of any animals on the farm. If a gate or a door was left open they went through and if nothing was left open they found a crack or hole; they could nip off a half-acre of young corn while you were driving them out, or they could sample a whole garden while you picked a few beans or dug a pan full of new potatoes for the next meal.

84

With all their devilment they were both beautiful and lordly as they marched, single file, with military precision down the path. There was something pathetic in their calls in response to their wild cousins who, in long lines winged their majestic flight over them spring and autumn. Often the tame ganders would answer the "honk, honk" from the skies or try out their powerless wings in a futile attempt to join their travelling kin.

When rain, sleet or snow kept the farmer out of the clearing he was busy mending for the coming season. First of all was his harness. It was all homemade but the bridle bits and trace chains. He usually killed a beef or two in the fall. He could take the hides to a near-by tannery—there was one in every neighborhood—and have them tanned on the halves. With his "side" of harness leather, his pegging awl and "waxed ends" it was no great job to make bridles, "britchen," back-straps and bellybands or cut hame strings. As a matter of fact this was an after-supper job, while the wife was spinning or knitting.

During the "glorious Fifties" each farm had four or five horses and an equal number of milk cows. The million odd stock cattle on the farms of Indiana found shelter around straw stacks or on the sheltered side of the barns. In any case there was a large accumulation of barnyard manure. The better class of farmers built a log pen twenty or thirty feet square and five or six feet high in which they placed the manure from the stables every week, and where it remained to rot for a half-year or more. This had to be hauled out onto the fields, spring and fall. Some farmers preferred to plow it under, some preferred to spread it on top of the ground after the crop was planted. Those who hauled it out directly from the stables usually plowed it under; those who rotted it in pens used it for top dressing. Either way it was a considerable job, which nobody particularly liked.

First of all came the garden. It had to be covered with manure and plowed as soon as the ground thawed in the spring. If manure was spread on the wheat it was done while the ground was frozen or, still better, when the snow was on. There were no manure spreaders and the work was done with a four-prong fork and a simple "twist of the wrist." If the manure on the corn land was not plowed under, it was placed, a half fork full at a place, directly on the hill of corn after the latter was planted and before it came up. This, of course had to be well-rotted manure. In any case hauling out the manure was no little job and it "spoke well" for a farmer to see his farm well covered with it, spring and fall.

The farmer's most important job in early spring was breaking for corn. The work began as soon as the ground was thawed. A side or turning plow was in general use, though a few of the more conservative farmers still used a big shovel plow, especially if oxen were used. During this decade, there was about one yoke of oxen in Indiana for each farm. The big gentle, lazy, liquid-eyed oxen were still in favor among the farmers. An ox team would break about an acre per day while horses or mules could break as much as two acres. All good farmers hoped to have their corn land, except the new ground, broken and harrowed by May 10. Planting was more rapid. The field was "laid off" with a one-

86

horse shovel plow into squares about three and a half or four feet and the corn dropped by hand in the intersections and covered with hoes. The dropping was often done by women, but men or grown boys handled the hoes. A planting crew usually consisted of one man and a horse to lay off the rows, and two droppers and two coverers with hoes. They planted about eight acres per day. Corn drills—not check rowers—were on the market but they were not favored because the farmers preferred to plow the corn both ways. Corn planting was finished by the middle of May and the new ground by the last of the month. If planting was finished in good time everybody had a holiday, usually spent in fishing.

There followed a busy month cultivating or plowing corn. All farmers hoped for a rain as soon as the planting was done and then two or three weeks of dry weather. Just as soon as the corn was up enough to show the row the alert farmer went over it with a "harrey" or harrow, removing the front tooth and straddling the row. Then at week or ten-day intervals he plowed it with a one-horse double-shovel plow. It is still undecided whether the crop should be "laid by"—that is, given the final plowing—with a shovel or a side (turning) plow. The latter left the corn ridged high and braced it against wind and storm. If a dry summer followed, however, it was just too bad. If two or three weeks of wet weather followed the planting, the weeds and grass "got the jump" on the corn and it had to be "barred" out. This meant weary days with the hoe. In any case the good farmer went over his cornfields after they were "laid by," or perhaps after harvest, and cut out all the weeds. This was done by the Fourth of July at latest, and we must now leave our cornfields for "harvest."

By the last of June the sun was riding high at its summer solstice, the wheat fields on the southern slopes were taking on a golden glow and the heavily whiskered heads were bending with the weight of the ripening grain. The farmer took down his grain cradle, sharpened the scythe, tightened the nib and mended the weak or broken fingers. Like the logrollings, wheat harvest was a neighborhood job, and required the united help of all the men, women and children. All other work waited because the wheat wouldn't; not even on Sunday. The hands began with the ripest wheat and changed from farm to farm, day by day as the fields ripened. It took from five to a

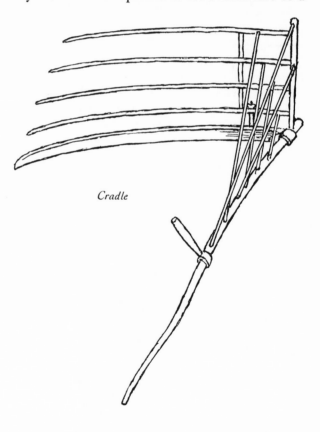

Cradle

dozen men. One shocker could keep up with two cradlers and two binders. The binders tied the bundles with bands of straw. At best the harvest lasted only ten days and an untimely wet spell meant heavy loss. Three acres was a good day's work for one cradler and a squad of five men usually shocked five acres of wheat.

In the logrolling the short, stocky men had the advantage, but in the wheat harvest the tall, deep-chested, rangy men were in their glory. Some trusty cradler set the pace, the others followed, each ten steps behind. Occasionally there were tests of endurance but sensible men would not risk the loss of a good hand by overwork to satisfy a foolish whim. Today we admire the endurance of a two- or four-mile runner but such activity is child's play compared to swinging a cradle in heavy wheat "from sun to sun."

After the spring work the winter fat was worked off and the men were in good training. The first swath in the morning sun started the sweat trickling down their faces and by ten o'clock there was little dry clothing. At the ends they met the water boy with a jug of fresh water from the spring. And how the barefoot urchin longed for the time when he could set his cradle down, reach for the jug with his left hand, flip it up on his shoulder and drink while he mopped his red, manly face with his right. "Gee! Only to be a man!" There were chicken, cake and pie on the dinner table and at ten in the morning and four in the afternoon the women brought out more pies and perhaps buttermilk for a short lunch under the shade trees. So the gay but tiresome work proceeded day by day from farm to farm until the wheat was all in shock. Then all

gathered in a circle, gave the "stubble call," re-
tired to the nearest swimming hole, performed
the necessary ablution, laid aside their sweaty
clothes full of prickly wheat beards, and wheat
harvest was over.

But the golden age of the cradler was passing.
Already at the county and state fairs McCormick
reapers were giving demonstrations before wide-
eyed and open-mouthed Hoosiers. The cradle
artist, who could leave the wheat stubble as level
as if it had been clipped by a modern lawn mower, was disgusted but the "machine" was on his
trail. The noblest art of the pioneer farmer was
lost to his own sons.

In 1856, middle of the "glorious Fifties," Indiana raised 9,350,971 bushels of wheat, about ten
bushels per head. This perhaps, was as much as
could be harvested by the cradle.

The farmer usually let his wheat stand in the
shock until the hay was cut unless an untimely
wind blew the shocks down. Then while the big
hay frame was still on the wagon he hauled the
wheat to the barn and stacked it. Sometimes he
stowed it away in the barn but it was much easier
and pleasanter to stack. Nobody wanted to get
up in the barn loft under the hot roof and put
away wheat, and then in a few days get up and
dig it out again when the thresher men came. The
days of the threshing floor and winnowing, as
previously practiced, had passed, and even the
"ground-hog thresher" was no longer used. The
horse power separator had taken its place.

Threshing was the most spectacular event of
the year. The "horse power" was a circular cog
machine driven by eight teams hitched to sweeps.
The power was carried to the separator by a long

*Hay
Fork*

Rake

90

iron rod, perhaps four inches in diameter, called the "tumbling shaft." The crew consisted of two drivers and two feeders, working in shifts of two each. The driver and the feeder were the heroes. Every distinguished visitor had to step up and feed a shift to show that he was a real man. The envy of the young boys was the driver who stood on a central platform, a long whip, the "stalk" about five feet long, in his hand. This would crack like a rifle and that was the signal for the horses to step off. The driver never dreamed of striking a horse with the whiplash. Instead, he sang to his teams in a monotone, much as the cowboys used to sing to the "dogies." His voice had to be raised above the general hum of the machine as he sang: "Jack, Jill, Kate, Bill, up here, up here!" followed by two or three short whistles. He kept one eye on the feeder who might signal for more power or stick up a finger to stop. The other eye was on the horses. Some horses were lazy and had to be encouraged; a limp or flinch indicated a sore foot or shoulder. So long as the sweat flowed freely and the white lather formed where the harness touched the hair, all was well, but when a horse quit sweating it was time to take him out. The driver could make a hit with a boy by taking him up on the platform for a "heat."

The other hero was the feeder. He took the bundles or sheaves one by one, shook them to pieces and fed them in so evenly that the gentle hum of the cylinder was never broken. A "chug" brought everybody to attention. It might mean an uncut band or wet wheat had gone through. About once in a season someone dropped a monkey wrench into the cylinder. The result sounded like a railroad crash; a dozen or so teeth were gone from cylinder and concave and the work was stopped for a half-day or so.

On the right of the feeder stood the band-cutter; two men laid bundles on the table before him; one or two pitched from the stack. An elderly man filled the half-bushel measure and kept the tally; a man poured the wheat from the half-bushel measure and two boys carried the wheat to the bins. Four or five men who took the straw from the separator screen finished the crew. The machines of that day had no strawstackers. The threshing crowd usually numbered not less than thirty and the food exceeded in abundance that for the logrollings. The older men consulted the tally to see what the "turn out" or yield was. Apparently the average for the state was about as at present, 18 to 20 bushels per acre.

Hay-harvest was unimportant in early Indiana. Some timothy and more redtop grew on the wet lands, yielding at best one ton per acre. This hay was cut right after wheat harvest with a light, long-bladed or mowing scythe. The mower had to bend over all the time making it tiresome on his back. An acre per day was good cutting. The scythe left the hay in a small windrow and if the mower was not careful a wisp of grass was left uncut at the end of each stroke. This made miserable work for the person who came along with a small hand or garden rake to gather the hay into bunches for the pitchfork, or to scatter it so the sun would cure it. When cured it was either built into shocks, "haycocks," or loaded on a sled and hauled to the mow. Much of it was stacked in the field, as you may yet see on many farms. Hay presses and mowing machines were coming onto the market as well as revolving horserakes. Red clover, now so common, was a novelty. It was considered good pasturage for stock cattle but would make horses "slobber" the same as white clover. If cut for hay there would be sure to be some ripe heads and the seed would "dry up" the milk cows. It was generally considered a good cover crop to turn under for wheat or corn.

The farmer had a breathing spell during the "dog days" of August. If he was "ornery" he hunted squirrels or loafed at the country store or blacksmith shop. If he was not "ornery" he "sprouted" the new ground, went through his cornfields with a hoe, or cut out the briers and weeds from his fence corners and pastures with the brush scythe. Poison ivy grew prolifically in the fence rows and those who were not immune often enjoyed a good case of ivy poison. This job of cutting the fence rows usually fell to the boys. Apparently all the hornets, "yaller" jackets, bumble-bees and wasps nested along the fences, and by the middle of the summer each nest was an enemy which no boy would pass up.

Those boys who were fortunate enough to live near the streams spent a large part of each day in the swimming hole. Curiously enough, girls were not permitted to go near a swimming hole. There were, of course, no bathing suits, and if there had been the sight of a woman in a bathing suit would have caused a panic in any neighborhood and mobilized every deacon in the township. A woman who could even swim was of doubtful character. She was not supposed to go fishing with her own brothers.

As soon as the fall rains had softened the ground the fall breaking for wheat began. A prelude to this was a week or so of manure hauling. The feverish rush of the springtime was over. All kinds of fruits were ripening and the women were busy making apple butter, drying apples, making marmalades, jelly and preserves. The horses were lazy from the green pastures, and all the folks were so full of food it was hard to keep in training. For two or three weeks the team or teams trudged slowly 'round and 'round the narrowing wheat field. The oxen with harrow or drag followed still more leisurely until the field was ready for the wheat drill or, more often, the sower. Many of the old farmers were still "skittish" of machinery and sowed the wheat broadcast. The children and turkeys chased the fat grasshoppers in the green meadows while the forest slowly put on its holiday dress of yellow and red. The fat frisky squirrels were cutting the hickory and beechnuts and spring chickens had passed through the frying stage. These were the "halcyon days" the poets speak of, unless the baby took the "summer complaint" or the older folks the "ager" or "fever" or granny came down with "yaller janders."

In the meantime the farmer had hauled his surplus wheat to the mill and either sold it to the "merchant miller" or had it ground and packed in barrels for the eastern or southern market. Store-keepers came back from the East about the first of October with a brand-new line of "hats, caps, boots and shoes," not to mention silks and satins, just beginning to rustle in Indiana society. A little later all climbed into the big wagon some bright morning and drove off to the big store to lay in the winter supplies. Real cash money was beginning to circulate among the folks. Homemade goods fell off one-half during the decade. "Store clothes," now ready made, soon crowded out the homespun, except with the deacons who mourned over the sinfulness and extravagance of the new times.

But the corn was ripening. The tassels and silks dried up, the "shoots" gradually bent away from the stalks and as they filled modestly bowed toward Mother Earth. If an early September frost did not play havoc, by the closing week of September the shucks were dry and corn was ready for the shock. The ordinary farmer cut eight or ten acres of fodder for his cattle during the winter. Nobody "hankered" for the job of cutting corn. It was hard, tiresome, uninteresting work. The dry blades cut one's wrists and neck until they were raw and bleeding; the big "woolly worms" crawled down under the worker's shirt and the sharp stubs skinned his shins as he staggered to the shock with a load of heavy fodder on his shoulder. No one who has not cut heavy corn all day knows how tired the left arm can become. No one came with a jug of water, no one brought pies and cakes to the field as in wheat harvest. The long V-shaped lines of wild geese "honked" on their way to Florida, the last mellow specimens of the Rambo, Yellow Belleflower, Maiden Blush and Carolina Sweets hung temptingly on the rapidly coloring apple trees, and all nature called from the near-by woods. But still the corn had to be cut on time. It was just plain work.

With the fodder in the shock and the wheat in the ground came the fall chores. The onions and potatoes, long ago lost in the wild grass, had to be dug out and placed in a cool place until freezing weather threatened. Then they were either "holed up" in the garden or stored in a dry part of the cellar, if such a part existed. The big late

95

Drumhead cabbages were through growing in October and a day was set aside when all hands made sauerkraut. If it were a German or Dutch family nothing less than four to eight barrels would do; otherwise a couple of barrels would answer. In any event it was at least an all-day job. The cabbages had to be pulled up, beheaded above the ears and the loose leaves carefully removed to get rid of all worms and traces of worms. Then the heads were placed in a big box which slid over three or four knives. After a few hours of vigorous "sawing" and salting and tamping one had a barrel of slaw which in time became "kraut." All this made the mouth water profusely. Surplus cabbages, onions or potatoes were given to less fortunate neighbors. No one thought of selling them.

Every farmer had an orchard and every orchard had from eight to twenty varieties of apples. The Early Harvests, Red and Yellow Junes, Summer Queens, Pearmains and Sweet Bows ripened in summer; those named previously ripened in the fall. During October the Imperial Winesaps took on a fiery red, the Baldwins became red-streaked, the Romanites speckled, the Russets golden and the Northern Spies a golden green. All had to be picked from the trees and carefully laid away in a dry cool place to season for the cellar or apple hole for winter use. The best were sorted out for this purpose and the remainder given to the neighbors or run through the cider mill— come to think of it, a glass of sweet cider along about nine o'clock on winter nights after one had either a dozen hickory nuts or walnuts was considered healthful.

There remained the corn husking. It might be husked on the stalk or snapped off and husked in

96

Apple Peeler

the crib shed—a husking bee, for instance. Whatever the procedure it has not changed with the
years. Tractors and gangplows have sent Buck
and Bright to the showers; the cultivator has put
the mules and double-shovel out of business; the
corn-cutter and shredder have superseded the
corn knife, but the champion corn husker of a
century ago no doubt would walk right along
with the champion of today—in fact Old Noko-
mis shucked Mondamin no differently. Human
ingenuity has not yet invented a machine which
can satisfactorily cut the weeds and grass from
the corn rows or husk the ripened corn on the
stalk.

The season ended—or began, according to the
weather—with hog killing or "butchering." We
may sing the praises of all the heroes of Indiana
from LaSalle or George Rogers Clark to the present, but the prosperity of our state through the
century has depended on Mr. Hog. In fat years
and lean years, until his late unmerited humilia-
tion (when he was ordered to be destroyed by
the government) he has come up with his part,
even though he does grunt about it consider-
ably. The hog population of the state during the
Fifties was about two and one-half millions, two
for each person, or a dozen for each family. Both
the day and the glory of the old "razorbacks"
were passing but stock hogs in general ran at large
and fed on the mast. During the summer when
the range was poor for hogs the prudent farmer
cultivated their acquaintance by giving them a
few ears of corn; or perhaps out in the lane he
prepared a slop trough where the hogs might
come and get the garbage and skim milk or a bas-
ket of bad apples.

About the tenth of December hogs selected for

97

the winter killing were penned up and fed corn for two or three weeks until they were fat enough to kill. As a rule they were two or three years old. On the appointed day three or four of the neighbors, each bringing "his old woman," gathered for the killing. Large kettles of water were heated to the boiling point, the water poured into large barrels or meat tubs set at an angle. The hogs were shot, one by one, stuck so the blood would drain out, then doused in the hot water until the hair was loosened, scraped with knives until free of all hair and dirt. Then tendons of the hind feet were raised, gambrel sticks inserted and the hog hung up on a pole so his nose was a foot or two from the ground. He was then gutted, the heart and liver hung up to dry, the leaf fat taken out for lard, the guts washed to be used as sausage casings. The Germans likely saved the blood for blood wurst which they stuffed in the hog's stomach after it was washed. As soon as the carcass dried it was carried into the smokehouse, where the head was cut off for "souse" and the body cut into shoulders, middlings (bacon) and hams, which left the knuckles, ribs and backbones for immediate use. Each neighbor returning home took enough "bones" to last a week. If the butcherings in the neighborhood were properly distributed each family might thus have fresh meat—spareribs, pigs knuckles and sauerkraut, or backbones—for a month. During this month the men put on the weight they had lost in harvest. Coming near the Christmas holidays it was a time of feasting.

The women's work did not vary so much with the changing seasons. The kitchen program was varied only slightly by the season's menu. Bread and meat came on the tables three times each day. The first garden vegetables, onions, lettuce and radishes, came in early in June and went out with frost. The first berries came in about wheat harvest and apples hung on the trees until November. From two or five milk cows had to be attended to morn and eve the year 'round; the milk was strained into crocks, in due time skimmed and the cream churned into butter and the skimmed milk served at table while still sweet, or made into cheese. As stated above, the wool furnished year 'round work. Early in the spring a dozen hens were set, half as many geese and a like number of turkeys. All these had to be nursed through the summer season.

Wash day monopolized one whole day each week and ironing and mending another. The children went barefoot half the year but it was no relief to mother. What time she saved in darning she lost in picking out briers and splinters and binding up misused fingers and toes. There was always someone ailing--"under the weather." Colds, sore throats, croup and winter fever were succeeded by summer complaint, sore eyes, chills and fevers. The mother was both doctor and nurse. And all this while she rocked the cradle with one foot. It took the Civil War to break this deadly monotony of women's lives but few mothers of the "glorious Fifties" lived to see the day.

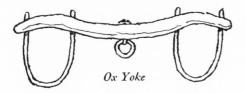

Ox Yoke

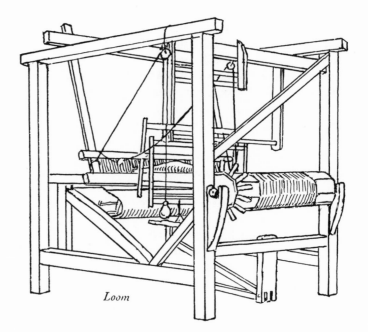

Loom

Waffle Iron

THE SETTLER BECOMES
A CITIZEN

The work of the first settler was not all done when he had cleared his little farm, built his log cabin, raised something to eat and made some clothing. Wherever he located he soon had neighbors. It is said that Daniel Boone moved out of Kentucky when another family located only ten miles from him. He felt that they were crowding him. The settlers of early Indiana were sociable and welcomed their neighbors; and neighbors came in mighty fast in those early years. Either before or soon after the settler located he went to the land office and bought his land. A record of these transactions can be found among the papers of the land department at the state auditor's office. As soon as he had finished paying for his land he got a deed and had it recorded by the county recorder. You may still find a copy of this deed at the county recorder's office. It usually took the settler about four or five years to pay for his land; so if you will subtract four or five from the dates of these deeds you will have the dates when these settlers located. The county assessor could show you how to make a map of the congressional or land survey townships. Perhaps he has them in printed form. On such a map one can mark the name, date and location of each settler. To make it more vivid one could use different colors for the different years, or better still, make a map for each year.

Bartholomew County will make a good example for the southern half of the state. Whitley is a good average county of the northeast or Benton, our baby county, in the northwest. There were no settlers in what is now Bartholomew County before the War of 1812. A roving band of Indians murdered twenty or thirty settlers along the southern edge in 1812 and scared all the others away. Three roads led up to this settlement from the Ohio River. One ran from Ash's Ferry and Madison, now state road seven. It took about a week for the settler to make his way over it in 1816. This county was known as the Flat Rock country and was recommended highly at Madison. Another road led up from Gwathmey's Ferry at Jeffersonville. It was called the Trader's Trace to the Pigeon Roosts, and was a nice level trail if the "cricks" were not up. It is now state road thirty-one. A third road came from the Ohio at Mauck's Ferry, by Corydon, Palmyra and Salem to the big Polk Patch around Brownstown. This is now state road one hundred thirty-five. It then took two weeks to "git up" from the river with a good ox team; now it takes about as many hours.

The first public affair that interested the settler was the militia. Although the poor Indians had learned at last that it was bad business to harm a settler they still roamed over this country, hunting. They were sullen and the settlers feared them. Every man had to join the militia and about

the first stranger who appeared at the new settler's door was the captain who had come to en-
roll him in the militia. This was the first law he
became acquainted with. It required him to have
a gun, a shot-pouch with a half-pound or so of
powder, thirty to fifty bullets, a good ramrod and
cleaning stick with a bunch of tow, bullet molds
and a hunting knife or hatchet. This last was
usually called a "tommyhawk." The captain took
the settler's name and age and told him when and
where to meet the other "boys" for training.
This meeting was always called the "muster" or
"training day."

The militia usually met twice a year, spring
and fall. In the spring there was the company
meeting—from forty to one hundred men under
a captain. In the fall all the men in the county met
as a regiment under a colonel. In the early days
there were always a few men in the neighborhood who had done some service in the Indian
wars, maybe in the Revolution or War of 1812.
The men elected their own officers and generally
chose such a man. The adjutant had a list of all
the men and as he called their names they took
their places in line. The captain then "inspected"
the men to see that each had what the law required. In the afternoon they might practice
marching through the woods, either in so-called
Indian-file, or the whole company abreast and
dodging from tree to tree. There was some tar-
get firing to see that each man's rifle was in good
condition and that he knew how to use it. The
men couldn't afford much of this practice, for
powder and lead were scarce. The most valuable
feature of these meetings was the renewing of
acquaintance.

These men were not strangers to the frontier or frontier ways. As one told about the Tippecanoe campaign, another told of the Pigeon Roost massacre; some had been with Harrison in Ohio, some with Jackson in Alabama, and those who had never seen an Indian had "hear'n tell." As they ate their lunches and passed the bottle, the stories grew more marvelous, the Indians larger and more ferocious and as Indians grew in size and number the more of them they killed. The poor Indian hadn't a chance and was slaughtered shamelessly. The new settlers, "strangers," were properly sized up as the "soldiers" gathered in little groups for the neighborhood gossip. If the womenfolks came, and they usually did, they traded out all their information along with their garden seeds and remedies for all kinds of ailments. Possibly someone in the neighborhood was sick or in need; if so, there were always volunteers to go to his aid. However the neighbors might gossip about one another, distress always made them equal. Altogether it was a great day in the new neighborhood.

The fall meeting was called the county muster or training day. It was no new thing. These folks had had it in England and had kept it up in the colonies and the states. It was held at the county seat and often lasted two days. If the October weather was nice the settler came in his wagon, maybe bringing something to trade at the store. Often the older settlers or perhaps candidates prepared a barbecue and the people who came from a distance brought blankets or skins to sleep on or under. This might be the only time during the year when friends from distant parts of the county would see each other and renew old acquaintances or make new ones. The work depended entirely upon the officers. If the officers were good ones, the men "fell in" at ten in the morning and actually trained until noon. Then they had two hours for dinner.

There was generally one company of mounted men in each county. All young men with good horses were eager to get into this outfit, for it was considered the best. They were called dragoons. If there should be a call to fight Indians these men would go first. They were supposed to be able to fire and reload their rifles from horseback.

Each captain tried to have his company make as good an appearance as possible for it was quite an honor to be elected a colonel. There were no uniforms, though occasionally the members of a company would have caps, belts or jackets alike. While the soldiers were drilling, the old men and women were visiting and sometimes the young people danced. It was a great time for candidates. As many as a dozen men would have papers recommending candidates and would be busy getting signatures. For ten or fifteen years this was the most important meeting of the year in each county. By 1830 few Indians were ever seen in the southern part of the state. The people forgot them and soon lost interest in the militia. By 1840 or 1850 the men ceased to bring guns with them and used cornstalks, placing corn tassels in their hats in imitation of the plumes then worn by soldiers in the regular army.

The first settlers had never used roads for hauling. What little produce they had for sale was carried to market on pack horses, driven on foot, or taken by boat. So when they settled in Indiana they usually built their houses off the trails. They soon learned they could not market corn or hogs on pack horses and that they had to open roads. Perhaps one settler in five came in a wagon. The United States Government gave the state three dollars out of every one hundred taken in at the land office but this was not enough to build many roads. If a number of settlers wanted a road they prepared a petition and gave it to the commissioners. These officers then sent three "viewers" to see whether a road was needed and, if so, they marked it off among the trees. The commissioners then ordered the supervisor of that road district to call out the "hands" and open the road. Not a dollar of money was spent on these "county" roads. The commissioners divided the county into road districts and over each district appointed a supervisor. Each man had to work on the roads at least six days each year.

So, sometime in summer or fall after the corn was "laid by," the supervisor would call at the cabin in the clearing and "warn" the man where and when to come to help make or mend a road. On the day named the settler took his axe, or his mattock, and started to perform his public duty. He received no pay, only a mark on the supervisor's little book to show that he had worked one day. Twelve hours, or "from sun to sun" was a day's work. Here, perhaps for the second time, he met all of his neighbors. After a week's work with them he began to feel as if he were acquainted.

First they cut all of the underbrush from the roadway. If a large tree, rock or other bad place was in the way, they just cut the road around it. The road did not have to be straight and it probably ran largely on government land. Along most of the way after the road was finished, the limbs of the larger trees overarched it completely. Sometimes, at the crossing of creeks, a bank would be dug down, just a little. If there was a wet place, a swamp or "drene"—a branch or small stream—the workers would cut poles, five or six inches in diameter and ten or twelve feet long, and lay them side by side to keep the wagon wheels or horses' feet from going down into the mud. At such places the driver had to keep his mouth shut to prevent his teeth from being jolted out. If a stream was small the road usually crossed at a gravelly ford, called a riffle. If the stream was too deep to ford, a quiet deep pool and a ferry was best. When the "cricks" were up wise people just didn't cross. Those who knew the stream swam their horses across and occasionally someone was drowned. The road was marked by "blazing" trees along the side. This made it plain to those who knew the neighborhood but strangers or travellers inquired at every house. As a rule settlers lived off the main road and each cut a side road up to his house. These "bye" or neighborhood roads were easily confused with the public road and the traveller often found his road at an end at a farmer's cabin. Roads built thusly were poor roads but the settler had enjoyed a week's visit with his neighbors and another tie had been woven around the little neighborhood community.

One afternoon a strange, barefoot, tow-headed boy of twelve walked slowly up the path to a cabin. After making friends with Towser he said his "mother reckoned as how you all might want to hear the preacher. He left a printment at Brother Blank's house over on the Paoli road just across Big Pizen (Creek) for a meetin' at early candlelight comin' next Wednesday. Mother hopes you all 'll come."

It was only three miles by the path through the woods, and on the appointed evening our pioneer folks left home about three o'clock and by dusk were at the meeting place. If it was nice warm weather the children all came—even the babies. These usually were asleep by preaching time, and were laid out of the way on blankets, old coats or anything handy. Even the loud preacher would not awaken them. By six o'clock there would be twenty grown persons present and meeting would begin. First, they would warm up with a psalm or hymn. The preacher would line it, that is, read the first line—"On Jordan's stormy banks I stand"—then they would sing that line. Then the preacher would read: "And cast a wistful eye"—and the folks would sing that line and so on —never omitting a stanza, if it took all night. For some reason they called this singing "billing." Our folks were accustomed to singing and some-one would remember the whole song from hear-ing it once and maybe next time the preacher came they could sing it without the "lining." In five or six cabins the following week one could have heard women humming or even singing these hymns as they went about their work. Some of them had beautiful voices; anyway there was no danger of disturbing their neighbors. There is no more beautiful picture of pioneer life than that of the mother with one foot on the cradle rocker softly singing "Oh, come, angel band, Come, come and around me stand," while she sewed, knit or darned. It is possible our awful "croon-ing" of today has come down from this practice.

I that speak
to thee am
he,

Next came the prayer. Like all things pioneer, no one could tell what it would be like. If it were some old Peter Cartwright he might roar like Goliath as he called down the wrath of a just God on guilty sinners or it might be as sweet and sad as the Sermon on the Mount as he pleaded for mercy for his children in the lonesome wilderness. Then, after another hymn, came the sermon, one or two hours long. The preacher usually stood in front of the fireplace with his Bible on a chair, if one could be found. The audience sat or stood in the little room, in the doorway, stuck their heads in the windows, or sat on the ground outside. All could hear, for as the preacher "warmed up," his voice rose until he could be heard a quarter of a mile. After the sermon they sang a doxology and if five or six church members were present, they organized a class and arranged for regular preaching. After a session of visiting the mother hunted up her baby and the father picked out one or two of the smaller children, took them under his arms or set them on his shoulders, and set out on the dark path for home. Many a youngster of ten who had been eager to come was not so eager on the return trip.

As the neighborhood grew, the men got together and built a log meeting-house—a chapel— down at the crossroads, by the creek, so they could have water handy for baptizing. Here the little group met for preaching, when they could find a preacher; here those that belonged to the same church (denomination) met as a "class" and talked over church affairs, perhaps sang, if someone could "lead"; here later was the Sunday school and here later were the blacksmith shop and country store.

After the work was over, the little group of

church members might decide to hold a camp meeting. It would bring folks from miles away and two, three or maybe four "big" preachers. Some Saturday in September the men gathered at the appointed place with axes and cleared off two or three acres for the campground; logs ten feet long and one foot in diameter, were cut and laid on cross logs the same size, for seats. Someone with a foot-adz dressed the bark and knots off the tops of the logs to make the seats as comfortable as possible. In front of the log auditorium they built a stand six or eight feet high, and perhaps ten feet square, for a speaker's platform. On the sides and at the back large heaps of dry logs and brush were piled to furnish light for the night meetings. A large space had to be cleared off for wagons and for cooking. There might be fifty or one hundred wagons. There was plenty of work, but the pioneers were not afraid of work. Everybody was supposed to bring his own food but not all of them did. Some came only to spend a day and stayed a week. All had to be provided for. When they got the grounds ready they prayed for nice weather and waited for the big day.

Preaching usually began at ten in the morning. By that time those who lived near, four or five miles, could be there, and those who camped could cook their breakfasts, water and feed their horses and "brush up." If there were three preachers, one spoke forenoon, one afternoon, and one at night. The sermons were long and powerful. After each sermon, exhorters or local preachers went up and down the walks urging the people to "jine" the church, while everybody sang or shouted. It usually took a day or two to get the meeting under full headway, but when it

did, it excelled any circus in interest. Sometimes a
great preacher—and some of the very best were
heard in Southern Indiana—held the large crowd
spellbound and silent for two hours—until scores
dropped to the ground from exhaustion. Sometimes a half-dozen "exhorters" would be shouting at the same time, like "barkers" at a street fair.
Sometimes a dozen would be praying at the same
time, some of them merely mumbling through
sobs and tears, others yelling like hussars leading a
cavalry charge. Sometimes when all was reason-
ably quiet someone would jump as high as he or
she could and yell "Glory, Glory, Glory, Uncle
Hiram or Aunt Jemima's got religion," maybe
repeating it a dozen times; and maybe Aunt
Jemima would rear right up from where she had
been on her knees and embrace the exhorter and
'round and 'round they would go as David
danced before the Ark of the Covenant.

Others would try to "shin it" up the trees to
get as near to heaven as possible. Sometimes, completely worn out, many would fall to the ground
either sound asleep or in a trance and have to be
carried away to keep them from being trampled
on. Sometimes the preacher would have to stop
in his sermon, get down from his scaffold pulpit,
join with other men and chase some drunken
rowdies away. The rowdies didn't always run,
and fists and clubs were used. The bootleggers,
then as now, always hung around with their jugs
and cups and many a scoffer who came for fun
and was made bold by too many drinks, found
himself tied hand and foot to a tree to listen to the
sermon. Long into the night the singing, exhort-
ing, praying and shouting continued until all were
tired out. Then the fires burned low, the folks

went home or to sleep in their wagons or under the big trees, the katydids and whippoorwills took up the singing, and the stars twinkled as usual. Ten or twelve men, selected for that purpose, kept guard over the camp. It was a great place for horse thieves to ply their trade. Nor must we forget that the young folks had a good time, the younger ones playing and the older ones caring for them and sparking as best they could. Men in small groups sat at a distance and talked politics or farming; candidates then as now were always on hand, especially attentive to the new settlers. Altogether it was the greatest social event of the year. As soon as the little church was organized the American Bible Society sent each family a Bible. This was often the first, and for many years the only, book in the house.

At the camp meeting one of the pioneer mothers had met an elderly neighbor who lived two or three miles away and who had spoken of a newspaper. One morning some days later, after her husband had gone to work, she called her ten-year-old son. "Do you mind the house way down the road at the foot of the big hill? Well, Miss Brown lives there. She was tellin' me they all git a newspaper from Vincennes. Comes down to the county seat and they go down every week or two and git 'em. You heered pa say how a man at the land office wanted him to take it but he didn't have any money left. Ken, you run down and ask Miss Brown fer the loan of it fer a day or two. I'll do your work this mornin'."

"I know where it is; Pa and I was past there t'other day squirrel huntin'."

"Now tell her yore name when you git down there, and where you live."

Some time later the boy arrived at the Brown cabin.

"Miss Brown, my ma wondered if you mightn't let her read your paper. She ain't had nothin' to read since we moved out here."

"Law, does yore ma read! I spec she gits right lonesome way up thar in the woods."

"Yep, course she works all day, but I hear her and pa talkin' after us childern has gone to bed and they wonder about things I don't know about."

"Well, well, come to think about it, I mind now I lent them papers to Squire Smith, last Sunday, two weeks past. Law, I thought he'd already brung 'em back. You know where he lives? Out on the Polk Patch road 'bout a mile; second house to the right. You kin just run by there and tell him I sed to let you have 'em. That's a little man."

"Ma said for me to say thank 'e."

"You tell yer ma to h'ist herself down this way sometime. I declare, here it is six month and she ain't never been to see me. You say yer Ma reads? Hain't you been to school yit?"

The question was too much for the boy. He had heard of schools but couldn't make out just what one was.

"They tell me Mis' Simpson is thinkin' of takin' in some scholars this fall. I hear'n she reads right peart. Some say she used to read out loud at a literary or something like that back where they come from. Her man, you know, preaches."

But the boy was hopelessly at sea and could only stammer a few "uh-huh's."

From the squire the boy got not one but four copies of the *Western Sun* and hurried home, proud of his adventures, for the squire was not too busy to ask all manner of questions about the new family.

That evening after supper, and after a small blaze had been kindled in the fireplace, the father stretched out lazily, half on the floor and half up against the log wall. The mother sat on a low stool, sidewise to the blaze, and the children nestled around, getting closer and closer as the mother read slowly, almost painfully picking out the words. It made no difference that the papers were two or three months old, and the advertisements were as interesting as the news about Bonaparte.

"Ma, where is them words you're sayin'?"

"Don't bother me, stir up the fire a little. I declare, I've plum near forgot how to read. John, don't you want to read awhile?"

"Naw, g'wan, you're gittin' better."

After an hour or so when the man apparently was asleep, the mother carefully folded up the papers and laid them away and the children curled up on the rude bed.

"John, I declare, you been listnin' to me any?"

"Some."

"I wouldn't a sent the boy away down thar for these papers if I hadn't thot you wanted to have 'em read."

"I shore am glad you got 'em."

"Did the children bother you?"

"Yep, I reckon they did, I reckon they did a heap."

"I didn't hear 'em; I was all busy with them words. Why didn't you speak to 'em?"

"Do you mind how Turk watches me while I gnaw the meat offen a bone at dinner?"

"Pa, wake up, air you clean gone asleep?"

"Wal, when that dog watches me that a way he wants somethin'."

114

"Pa, you think more of that old dog than you do of me and the children, I do believe."

"Yassir, that dog wants somethin', and that boy wants somethin', and he wants it worser than the dog wants a bone. Come Sunday you put on yer good bonnet and h'ist yerself on the critter and we'll take these papers down to where you got 'em. I hearn Brown sayin' somethin' about a woman going to teach someplace this fall but I didn't listen much."

The men did not show as much interest in a school as they had in a church but finally ten or twelve children were subscribed and the wife of a local preacher agreed to teach them. There was no money to be had but the teacher was paid in corn, meat and other produce. They added a mud and stick chimney to the log "chapel" and used it for a schoolhouse. School began about the first of September and lasted until the middle of October. After that the weather was too bad for the children to go so far through the woods.

There were no classes in this school. Each "scholar" had his own work. Most of them had no books. Our scholars in the cabin had alphabet morning, noon and night. Their first work was to learn to say it without mistake or hesitation. Then they began their word-making and spelling; A, b, ab; e, b, eb; i, b, ib; o, b, ob; and u, b ub; then b, a, ba; b, e, be; b, i, bi; b, o, bo; and b, u, bu until they had learned all these combinations. By the end of the six weeks a ten-year-old boy was slowly but very delightfully spelling out and reading with many strange pronunciations the simple stories of the Bible—his only reader. In the meantime, boys and girls had perfected their counting, had learned the addition and subtraction tables, but were hopelessly stalled by "carryin' " in addition and "borrerin' " in subtraction. Next year they would have a book—maybe a speller or maybe a reader—and learn to write. In three six-weeks terms they would read, write and cipher and be ready to meet the big world on even terms.

Our typical pioneer had probably had but little practice in local government and politics until he moved to Indiana. A squire and a constable were all the officers he knew outside of the militia. So when in the late summer he rode down to the county seat he heard much strange talk and saw some strange sights. The county seat town had a log courthouse with two rooms. Around it was a yard about three hundred feet square cleared of underbrush. Over on the corner of the large lot was a heavy log pen some twelve by twenty feet with only a heavy puncheon door. This, he was told, was a jail. By the side of the jail and running along the road was a little patch of ground about twenty feet wide and fifty feet long, a man sitting at one end with a rifle and another man walking back and forth in the small space. This man, he learned, was a prisoner, walking for exercise. When he became tired, and at night, he would be locked in the little log jail.

Even before the settler came out of the woods he had heard someone shouting much as the preacher did at the camp meeting. One room of the courthouse he found packed full of people and a man at one side talking as if the world were coming to an end. A rather important looking man, with his long hair combed back over his shoulders, sat facing the crowd, and on the front log were twelve men in a row. He found out shortly that this was what they called the circuit court. The man sitting in front was the judge, the men in a row were the jury and the man talking so loud was a lawyer. He had always heard it was best to keep out of court so our visitor didn't stay long.

Across the road from the courthouse was the store, a little one-room log house. A bag of green coffee, a bushel or so of salt, some plug tobacco, a can of gunpowder, some bars of lead, a can of tea, two or three hoes without handles and about the same number of axe-handles with axes, composed his stock. In a box were five or six letters and three or four newspapers. The newspapers were not wrapped and perhaps never had been. This, then, was the United States post office. There was no regular mail carrier yet but the postmaster at Salem sent the mail up when he had a chance.

While the newcomer was chatting with the postmaster an elderly man came in and introduced himself as the treasurer of the new county. He asked our settler if he had been listed.

"I dunno what you mean," replied the latter, "but I reckon not, leastwise not as I know on."

After asking where he lived and where he came from, how long he had been there and how was he comin' on, the treasurer said he would send the "lister" around to see him.

"You'll be clearin' a passel of new ground come fall and winter most likely?" inquired the treasurer.

"I calkilate on't," returned the settler.

"Be needin' any help?"

"Not as I knows on."

"You know this man Glack, squatted over toward Big Injun's, had the shakes all spring and summer and was turned 'vagrant' on us. We're havin' an auction over at my place on t'other side the square this evenin'. Thought as how you might want to bid on 'im."

"Could shore use him and got plenty of grub, but I reckon I couldn't find anywhere he could sleep."

The treasurer was also serving as overseer of the poor and that afternoon our settler saw the unfortunate man sold to a man who agreed to give him food, shelter and clothes and pay him a small amount if he got able to work. The contract was to last for a year. At the same time two little children who had been left homeless were "sold out" to the lowest bidder to take care of for the "time bein' " until homes could be found or until someone would "take 'em to raise."

When the sun was about an hour high the loud talking at the courthouse ceased, the folks separated into little groups, everybody talking to everybody else. Finally our settler, as folks began to leave, got on his horse and rode slowly away to his cabin home.

He had not long to wait. One afternoon the following week the lister, a rather active middle-aged man, rode up and "halloed" the house. The settler invited him to "light and hitch your nag."

"Nope, no use, just want to talk a spell," said the stranger as he dismounted and passed his arm through the bridle reins. "I hearn you be a new-comer and I kim by to list ye. Yer name? How old might ye be? Uh huh. How much land did ye enter? Uh huh. Paid fer? No tax on yer land till four years after it's paid fer. Any hoss beast? Uh huh; one critter. No other beasts? No. Come next spring yer tax'll be, poll fifty cents, critter tax ten cents. Pay ter the treasure next May."

So our settler was enrolled as a taxpayer.

For an hour or so the men talked of neighborhood affairs, of old times, those who had been there the previous year or longer, of newcomers, those who had moved in that season, of sickness, of the weather, of growing crops and finally of politics.

"I reckon as how you all ha' hearn about the big 'lection this fall?"

"Naw, not much. I been so busy cuttin' sprouts and workin' the corn I just ain't give no heed. I mind now as I did hearn some talk down at the meetin'."

"Ye been hearin' about Andy Jackson?"

"No."

"Mr. Potts ut lives down on Musky was over at Salem to the big convention. He said Jackson was the man fer president. When the Indians was cuttin' all kinds o' capers down in the South Old Andy gethered up a posse of men from Tennessee and marched down into Alabam'e and jist naturally cleaned them varmints out. Guess he must o' killed thousands of 'em. They say the woods air full of 'em up state. We got to get rid of 'em and Old Andy'll do it."

"I dunno," returned our settler, "they ain't never harmed me. Course, I don't like 'em any better'n you do. They was a passel of 'em by here yisterday; ragged, dirty, hungry looking. I give 'em a hand full o' salt and the woman cooked 'em a pone o' bread. Seemed to do 'em a power o' good."

"That's the way o' them varmints, I tell you," broke in the lister. "Can't put no 'pendence on 'em. They come draggin' their lips around yer in daytime ter see what ye got and then come back

119

at night un git it. They tell me they do have a sight o' hoss critters to sell the traders up Fort Wayne way. Leastways it's peculiar like when they don't raise none nor buy 'em. They say the President has done sent soldiers down to Georgia t' pertect Injuns from the settlers. Don't that beat ye? Jo Potts said he hearn, too, down to the convention at Salem, if Jackson was elected he'd turn all the rich men out of office and give 'em to the pore men like you and me and most likely we'd have free land fer the settlers; specially fer the squatters. That ud help the western country powerfully. Jackson's shore a friend to the pore man. Ken I put ye down fer Jackson?"

"I dunno," drawled the settler. "I've dun contracted fer my land and I shore ain't hankerin' fer any office. It does seem bad to drive these pore Injuns out uv the only home they got. There's right plenty o' huntin' yit in these woods. But I cain't say as the women folks wants 'em strollin' around, though. I guess I'll go fer Jackson."

Late in October when the trees had put on a riot of red and yellow our settler and his family started at daybreak and went over to the county seat to a rally of Jackson men. It seemed everybody was there. They took corn pone and venison quarters, and wild turkeys simmered over the hot coals. General John Carr, who had lately bought land in the county, spoke from twelve o'clock until two. After he had finished some speakers, called "rabble-rousers," continued as long as anyone would listen.

This was just a beginning in politics. That fall the county commissioners divided the county into townships and in the spring trustees, secretaries, treasurers, fence-viewers, stray-keepers,

THE SETTLER BECOMES A CITIZEN

poor overseers, road supervisors and school trustees, were to be elected. In the summer or early fall county and state officers had to be elected. It seemed everybody and everybody's friends were candidates. But here we must leave our settler. With the opening of spring he became an old-timer. He was now really a citizen of Indiana.

Rocking Chair

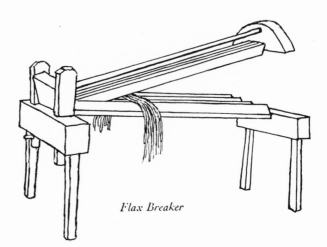

Flax Breaker